Behold,
Believe,
Become

"Cultivating an authentically Catholic religious imagination is a necessary foundation for learning to pray the Mass so that it is truly life changing every time. I am thrilled by Timothy O'Malley's sometimes playful and always reverent contribution to this critical work at this time in Church history. *Behold, Believe, Become* instills an awe and wonder that will lead you into the heart of worship. Praise God!"

Sr. Alicia Torres, FE
National Eucharistic Revival executive team member

"O'Malley is a deeply faithful, kind, and wildly smart man. Reading his new book *Behold, Believe, Become* was like sitting with a friend before Mass and chatting about the beauty and depth of everything we could see, hear, and begin to feel. The Mass can be intimidating, at times foreign, and even jarring, but O'Malley's explanation of the tactile, physical things within our worship helps bring Mass to a place of familiar comfort and rich beauty. This book is essential reading in these months of Eucharistic renewal and long beyond because it will spark a personal revival within your heart and push you to be at Mass with open eyes, a hungry mind, and a ready heart."

Katie Prejean McGrady
Host of *The Katie McGrady Show*
on The Catholic Channel on Sirius XM

"*Behold, Believe, Become* is a summons to experience the Eucharist as a mystical moment where the divine meets the human in the fullness of our embodied existence. As the pages turn, the senses are extraordinarily drawn into seeing, tasting, smelling, hearing, and touching all matter related to the Eucharistic miracle."

Hosffman Ospino, PhD
Professor of theology and religious education in the
School of Theology and Ministry at Boston College

"If you've never understood what all the 'smells and bells' at Mass are for, then this book will spark your sense of wonder. O'Malley, like a masterful tour guide, pauses at the most ordinary objects and motions during Mass and helps us to see their extraordinary realities."

Tanner Kalina
Author and evangelist

"This terrific writer and true believer has done it again! These insightful, profound, and sometimes playful reflections on the source and summit of our faith—Sunday Mass—help us encounter Jesus and our deepest selves in the concrete stuff of the Eucharist. Never again will you see doors, water, altars, bread, or burning flames quite the same way."

Fr. Joe Laramie, SJ
National director of the Pope's Prayer Network
and author of *Love Him Ever More*

"In *Behold, Believe, Become*, O'Malley is courting the modern Catholic heart to contemplation within the Holy Mass. It is a wooing of the human heart, wounded by our own inventions, to sit at the feet of Jesus and ponder his magnanimous love in the Eucharist. It is a persistent pursuit of the vagabond within us and invites us to become mystics."

Fr. Agustino Torres, CFR
Founder of Corazón Puro

Behold, Believe, Become

Meeting the Hidden Christ
in Things We See, Say, and Do at Mass

An Unconventional Look at Eucharistic Worship

Timothy P. O'Malley

McGrath Institute for Church Life | University of Notre Dame

AVE MARIA PRESS AVE Notre Dame, Indiana

Nihil Obstat:	Reverend Monsignor Michael Heintz, PhD
	Censor Librorum
Imprimatur:	Most Reverend Kevin C. Rhoades
	Bishop of Fort Wayne–South Bend
	Given at Fort Wayne, Indiana, on 15 December, 2023

The *Nihil Obstat* and *Imprimatur* are official declarations that a book or pamphlet is free of doctrinal or moral error. No implication is contained therein that those who have granted the *Nihil Obstat* or *Imprimatur* agree with its contents, opinions, or statements expressed.

Founded in 1865, Ave Maria Press is a ministry of the United States Province of Holy Cross.

www.avemariapress.com

Paperback: ISBN-13 978-1-64680-338-5

E-book: ISBN-13 978-1-64680-339-2

Special Edition product number: 30016

Cover images © De Agostini Editorial / Getty Images and ABAZAKIS / iStock / Getty Images Plus.

Cover design by Kristen Hornyak Bonelli.

Text design by Brianna Dombo.

Printed and bound in the United States of America.

Library of Congress Cataloging-in-Publication Data is available.

*To Fr. Romano Guardini,
whose writings have taught me to see.*

CONTENTS

INTRODUCTION

Walking through a shopping mall in the 1990s, you unavoidably came upon one of those Magic Eye puzzles. For those readers who are not citizens of Generation X or older millennials, Magic Eye puzzles appeared initially as a mishmash of colors, lines, and shapes. They looked like bad modern art, generated on a computer with minimal graphic capabilities. But if you stood before the image and relaxed your eyes, a hidden object would suddenly appear to you. Out of the jumble of colors and shapes, there would be a cat wearing a top hat. A bear eating salmon next to a river of cheese. Michael Jordan dunking a basketball (it was the nineties, after all). With a slight adjustment to *how* one looked at the image, a hidden message was revealed to those who could see it.

The rub was that not everyone could see it. It took practice. You could not see the hidden image through mere exertion of the will. Everyone had stories of friends (for what is a trip to the mall without meandering around with friends?) who stood there for half an hour to no avail. Often, they were trying too hard. To really see what was hidden, you had to stand in front of the picture and relax, letting your eyes

move out of focus, ironically, so that you could see. Magic
Eye viewing required a formation into the right kind of visual
habits so that you might see the hidden made present in the
visible.

I always think about Magic Eye puzzles when I read the
following sentence from the Church's Constitution on the
Sacred Liturgy from the Second Vatican Council, *Sacrosanctum Concilium*: "But in order that the liturgy may be able to
produce its full effects, it is necessary that the faithful come
to it with proper dispositions, that their minds should be
attuned to their voices, and that they should cooperate with
divine grace lest they receive it in vain" (*Sacrosanctum Concilium*, no. 11). The Catholic Church makes a lot of claims
about our worship. In the Church's liturgical celebrations,
Jesus Christ comes to act among us as the risen Lord. He
becomes present to us, speaks to us, and makes his saving
deeds available to every generation. But if you look at what
you see before you, that's not immediately what you behold.
Rather, you see a priest wearing funny clothes. You perceive
a bunch of people singing so out of tune that you imagine it
must be on purpose. During Mass, you notice what seems
like nothing more than a rather thin piece of bread being
held up by the priest wearing the odd clothes.

But there's more to see if you look closely. That priest is
the person of Christ, acting among the People of God to offer
the sacrifice of Christ for the life of the world. That singing
is the loving presence of Christ, who has emptied himself to

dwell among us through the poverty of our voices (and how poor they often are!). That thinnest of all pieces of bread is, in fact, the Body of Christ, our Lord coming to feed us. We see none of these things routinely. Instead, we must come to this worship with the proper dispositions so that worship may be fruitful, so that we can see more than what the naked eye alone beholds. That's the disposition we need.

The word *disposition* may be one that you are unfamiliar with. Another word for "disposition" is *habit*. A baseball player possesses certain habits or dispositions that he has honed throughout his play of the game. He knows almost unconsciously the right force needed to make a throw from third base to first base. He does not blindly swing at every pitch but has studied the tendencies of pitchers. He has practiced the proper stance and motion needed for an effective swing. He does this without consciously thinking about what is required. It is habitual. He has those dispositions proper for a baseball player. Lacking those habits, our imagined baseball player will find the game of baseball difficult, boring, and likely a waste of time.

Catholics require dispositions for worship akin to the baseball player. *Sacrosanctum Concilium* highlights the most essential of these dispositions. We need to be able to attune our minds with our voices. To engage in the liturgy fully, consciously, and actively, we need to perceive the deeper meaning of what we are doing. Of what we are beholding. Of the ways that we use our bodies in worship. We need to abide in a space of faith, hope, and love in our worship.

Now, let me be clear. In saying that there is a deeper meaning, I don't mean that there is a single meaning—a one-to-one correspondence. I once took a youth group to see a film adaptation of C. S. Lewis's *The Lion, the Witch and the Wardrobe*. We went to a coffee shop afterward to discuss the movie. Our well-intentioned students, almost at once, fell into examining the film as a series of hidden meanings that, once unlocked, led you to understand the secret overall "meaning" of the film. The lion is Christ. Susan is Judas. The film, in essence, could have been more easily told through a chart identifying each character with someone from the gospels. After viewing the chart, why even watch the movie?

Instead, I refer to "meaning" as *logos*. Okay, you were probably hoping not to read a single Greek word in this book. Alas, the seal has been broken. But it will be worth it, I promise.

Remember that in the very first chapter of Genesis God created the world through speaking words—in Greek, *logoi* (the plural of "word" in Greek). When God spoke these words, God revealed something about himself. In everything that was created, God gives meaning (*logos* refers not only to a word but also meaning). The glory of a sunset over the Pacific Ocean. *Praise him.* The scrunchy face of a newborn babe. *Praise him.* An elderly couple holding hands while sitting on a bench. *Praise him.*

The world, as the Church Fathers often reminded us, consists of *logoi* of the *Logos*. They are words that reveal something about the Word. The Father speaks a word, and that Word is the Son. The Word, as St. John's gospel reminds us, who became flesh, restoring us to his image and likeness. The enfleshed Word, Jesus Christ, who revealed to us that God has an ultimate meaning for each of us, if only we have the eyes to recognize it.

This is why the Church took up the natural world in her worship of this wondrous Creator God. Light and darkness. Water and oil. Bread and wine. Hands extended, torsos bowed down, kneeling and standing. All these are *logoi* of the *Logos*. Little words about the Word. Little words that possess meaning. Little words that Jesus himself used throughout his ministry.

Fruitful worship, therefore, means contemplating the meaning of all these little *logoi* or words. The language of contemplation is chosen quite intentionally. Contemplation is not an obscure activity exclusively for monastics and vowed members of religious communities alone. Rather, contemplation means *beholding*. It means taking time to look at what we do, why we do it, and what it could mean for us worshippers of the triune God. Why do I walk through a door into a church? Why do I stand to listen to the Gospel at Mass? Why are churches often full of the light of stained-glass windows?

It shouldn't surprise us that our God—who is a wonderful teacher of us mere mortals—has employed many of these embodied, meaningful actions in sacred scripture. A principle of Catholic theology is that nature is perfected by grace. God uses light and darkness, processions and eating, water and deserts, gates and smoky incense to save men and women throughout sacred history. In this sense, the meaning of what we do in worship has been revealed not only in creation but in God's unfolding plan of redemption for us.

This book, therefore, seeks to initiate us worshippers into the proper dispositions necessary to adore fruitfully the living God who created and redeemed the world. The created order consists of *logoi* of the *Logos,* words about the Word, who came to redeem us using the very *logoi* that revealed him from the beginning. This book will contemplate the *matter* of the liturgy. Water drowns, and it quenches thirst. Quite naturally, it's used in Baptism, and it is placed at the door of each church as we enter. We drown our sins, and we thirst for the living God.

If there's a motto for this book, it's something I've told my students for years: matter matters. For this reason, I will provide an unconventional walk through the Mass. We won't be dealing with the history of Eucharistic Prayers, what the texts say about God, or the history of Eucharistic doctrines. Rather, we'll be dealing with the stuff of Eucharistic worship—the things we see, say, and do—from the time that we enter the church to the time that we depart at the end of Mass.

This book is dedicated to Fr. Romano Guardini (1865–1968), the German Catholic priest who is the impetus behind the methodology of this book. It is dedicated to this now-deceased priest (who I believe is a saint) because everything that follows is a shadowy imitation of what I have learned from Fr. Guardini in his *Meditations on the Mass* and his *Sacred Signs*. Readers who are familiar with his social commentary on time, power, and technology will see resonances throughout. If you find this book fruitful, make sure to turn to Fr. Guardini himself.

If I might be so presumptuous, at least on the part of Fr. Guardini, I ask his prayers for us. The seemingly endless liturgical wars after the Second Vatican Council must eventually come to an end. And if that's going to happen, it will be because we return to the roots of what Fr. Guardini hoped the reformed rites could do for us—help us to abide as contemplative, liturgical, and sacramental creatures in a world governed more by technique and power than by wonder. And, therefore, to reshape this world of ours according to a liturgical and sacramental way of being, rather than one defined by politics and economics alone.

This is not a book meant to be read straight through. Rather, it presupposes that the reader wants to exercise his or her sacramental vision. The exercises at the conclusion of each small chapter beckon the reader to a threefold work: *Behold:* look again at how you use your body both in the world and in worship. *Believe:* ponder how this chapter's sign might lead you into deeper communion with the Beloved, transforming your life in the process. *Become:* commit yourself to practices that foster a way of seeing that changes how you do everything.

This book is the last in a trilogy that I have written loosely connected to the USCCB's Eucharistic Revival of June 2022 to June 2025. The first, *Real Presence: What Does It Mean and Why Does It Matter?* (Ave Maria Press, 2021), presented the pastoral wisdom of the doctrines of Real Presence and transubstantiation. The second, *Becoming Eucharistic People: The Hope and Promise of Parish Life* (Ave Maria Press, 2022), sought to inspire in the parish practices that lead to a deeper appreciation of the Eucharistic nature of the Church and our vocation to transform every crack and crevice of the cosmos. This third is concerned with the kind of vision we need to foster in order to become Eucharistic creatures whose lives are defined by worshipful wisdom.

Across all three, you will see a robust, Christo-centric, and socially conscious vision of evangelization—not just inviting people to come to Mass, but fostering cultures in parishes, neighborhoods, and schools grounded in the Eucharistic mystery of the Church. If there is to be a renewal of Church life, one must attend to the social consequences of the Eucharistic mystery—the way that being a Eucharistic person changes how I think about human life as a whole in community with my neighbor. Lacking this social context, the individual believer may come to a more profound faith in the Eucharistic Lord, but such faith may be lived privately apart from how we educate, work, use money, order our time, and participate in the creation of cultures grounded in the self-giving love of Christ rather than in power, technique, and prestige.

Let's get started by practicing the new way of seeing that this book sets out to teach—changing how we understand and do everything—by taking a fresh look at the cover of this very book. Perhaps with eyes newly focused you may behold deeper meanings than you at first perceived. If matter matters, as this book claims, then so do the very material realities depicted on the covers of books including this one. The arresting cover design by Kristen Hornyak Bonelli, creative director at Ave Maria Press, has a meaning, which the reader might not immediately recognize. The abstract geometric shapes on the cover are inspired by floors in the cosmatesque style of inlay stonework typical of the architecture of medieval Italy and especially Rome. If you visit Rome today, you can still see this style in many churches there. These floors were intended to represent the pilgrimage that each Christian undergoes as they take up a journey toward the altar of God. The stones were often gathered from all over the world, and through them, all the cosmos and history itself were taken up into Christian worship.

Now, notice that in the cover design, when you let your gaze move inward, you see Jesus Christ. You see the Eucharistic Host, the presence of God that helps us recognize all

those other presences. In brief, you see Christ hidden there
beyond the words of the book's title. I hope by looking at
this image and reading this book, you grow to appreciate all
the more the cosmic consequence and profound meanings of
the Mass. I know that Kristen's design invited me to behold
and believe anew when first I saw it. May you also find unex-
pected understanding there.

So, let's behold the wondrous mystery hidden in the *stuff*,
the *matter*, of the Mass. Take your time working through the
book. There are questions to guide you at the end of each
chapter and links to short videos featuring my own voice and
personal reflections from Rachel and Jason Bulman of *Meet
the Bulmans*. Return as often as you like to each chapter, for
upon second and third and fortieth readings, there will be
even more to see.

1.

THE RISING SUN

Sunday morning just feels different.

Monday through Friday, the O'Malley household awakens with a start. Preparing school lunches. Cajoling children into brushing teeth and putting on clothes. The weekdays are a time measured by productivity, by how much we can get done before the school bus arrives. And it never feels like we can do it all—it's as if we're always squeezing in one last task before the workaday world overwhelms our predawn, slumbery dreams. Morning turns into afternoon, which fades into evening, which becomes about homework and showers and once more going to bed, so that the next day, we can get up and do it again.

Saturday isn't about productivity. There are no alarms to set, no immediate preparations to be made. It's a day of leisure, a time for pure delight—for cinnamon rolls and cartoons and (maybe) showering. Yeah, there's an activity or two—a dance class here, a soccer game there. In the early days of autumn, there's college football to attend to. When the last whistle blows in late fall, our attention turns to hikes and maybe a trip to an indoor pool. Ultimately, Saturdays are for nothing and therefore for everything.

Sundays, as I already said, are different. The leisure of Saturday overflows into the first moments of Sunday. With the piercing rays of the sun's light, we arise from our beds. We savor those first and second cups of coffee. But unlike the meandering pace that Saturday persuades us to adopt, there's something to do. It's time to go to Mass.

It's funny how that decision to go to Mass changes everything about Sunday. We talk about the weekend as a time separated from the weekdays by the absence of school and work (at least for those lucky enough to have a weekend), but that familial commitment to worship the living God alongside our neighbors on a Sunday leads to a different experience of time. Yes, the Mass is something that we have to do (there is an obligation of justice to worship God every Sunday for a Catholic). We could even put it on our schedule if we wanted to. But something about listing Mass on our Google calendar doesn't feel right. Do we put thirty minutes of cuddling with our beloved on our calendar? Calendars are for things like meetings, classes, or after-school extracurriculars. But is Mass just checking off a box, the same thing as showing up to our haircut appointment or picking kids up from school?

It raises the question: What are we really doing at Mass? You might be surprised to hear that we are doing nothing. Now, let's be clear. I don't mean that God isn't worth our time. In fact, contrary to our addiction to frenetic productivity, maybe God is the only thing that is worth giving our time to in the first place. But whatever we're doing at Mass, it's not considered all that important by the titans of industry, the creators of culture, and the politicians wielding power. No money is made. No culturally important artwork comes into existence. State craft is not practiced. Mostly ordinary folks are just trying to worship God. For this little bit of time, we let God take over.

I suppose this is why I remain entranced by the early rays of dawn on a Sunday morning. Right before the sun ascends upon the Indiana plains near my house, there is nothing but darkness. Darkness is the realm of chaos, of the unknown and terrifying—bears and wolves and monsters that lurk in those spaces and places unseen by human sight. When I was young, I would sit in my room and imagine what lurked out there, convincing myself that there existed terrors no mortal tongue could tell. But with the first rays of dawn, the darkness departs—and alongside it, the fears. Light has come.

It makes sense, therefore, that early Christians understood the rising sun as a symbol of the advent of Jesus Christ. Into the world of darkness came the Light to all the nations, the Daystar from on high who scatters the darkness of despair, sin, and death, as well as all the monsters that prowl in the shadows, lurking to bring about their despicable plans. Into that world came Jesus Christ. And now every morning—Sunday or not—we remember the wondrous mystery of this advent. The sun rises. We remember that Christ comes into this world, not just once upon a time, but this morning.

So, when we rise, awakened by the rising sun on Sunday morning, we are engaging in a prophetic assault against productive time—a measure of time that is only concerned about accomplishment, about removing things from our to-do list (only, of course, to have more to do later). As we wake up and get ready for Mass, we're giving *all time* back to God, who is the Creator, Redeemer, and Sanctifier, not of some abstract world out there, but of our world here and now.

We are letting our time enter into God's time. And isn't that what the kingdom of God is about in the first place? The plans of mere mortals involved in the serious business of the workaday world look so small compared to what God has planned for us. We call that plan heaven itself, the moment in which all time will be defined by God's eternity rather than by our own idolatrous productivity. It's what we are practicing every Sunday morning—learning to feel comfortable with heavenly time.

So, I say, let us arise with that Sunday morning sun. Let us go about that leisurely business of worshipping the triune God. And rather than let that Sunday worship remain but a single moment on our calendar, let that time of praise, adoration, and thanksgiving become the defining moment of all time. With every rising of the sun, remember: we are creatures measured not by the time clock or the digital calendar but by the God who entered time, dwelling among us. Let the heat of the sun that drives away the darkness and frigidness of the world spill over into every moment of every day. "In the heavens he has set a tent for the sun, which comes out like a bridegroom from his wedding canopy, and like a strong man runs its course with joy. Its rising is from the end of the heavens, and its circuit to the end of them; and nothing is hid from its heat" (Ps 19:4b–6). If we recognize this fact, we might learn to dwell in the presence of God, not only in that constricted hour on a Sunday morning, but all the time.

Behold, Believe, Become

1. Think about your relationship with time. Do you feel busy? Is your time defined mostly by productivity? Why is or isn't this the case?

2. The rising of the sun has traditionally been a symbol of Christ's own conquering of darkness, of a time defined by terror and frigidity rather than warmth. Where in your life do you need the light of Christ's presence? Where do you need to live by a different accounting of time?

3. How might you better let the worship that you do on Sunday morning have an effect on the rest of your week? What practices might you take up to shape a new relationship with a time defined not exclusively by productivity but by worship?

Scan this code or visit **http://www.avemariapress.com/behold-believe-become-videos** to watch a video from Tim O'Malley and the Bulman family on meeting Christ in the rising sun.

2.

THE DOOR

Most of us don't reflect very often on the objects that we encounter throughout any given day. We don't have the time to do so. We get up in the morning, jump into our cars, turn on the music, rush to our jobs, go into our buildings, spend eight hours in front of a computer or working on a factory floor, go home, and do it all again. If you exclusively gazed upon the beauty of the sky as you drove, or reflected deeply on the gift of a particular coworker, you'd be late to work or you'd be behind in what needs to be accomplished. Wondering is for those leisurely few who have the time to do so. For the rest of us, there are tasks. And the objects in our lives are merely the setting for our productivity. Cars. Buildings. Desks. Stuff that we relate to as we go about the mundane drama of living.

And that's well enough. You could imagine a world where we spend so much time looking around, wondering at our slice of the cosmos, that no one would get fed. No one would clean their living room or build a new house. People wouldn't get married or have children, because they would be lost in thought. There would be a bunch of people wandering around the world, their eyes fixed upon some object, bumping into one another like wonder-filled zombies.

But you can become a zombie in another way too. You could so forget the beauty of the world that you never take a moment to pause before the myriad of wonders to behold. Your relationship to the world could become utilitarian. Houses aren't homes, just places to go to sleep at night. Cars aren't tremendous machines, just ways to get from point A to point B. People aren't individual persons worth talking to and collaborating with, but forces that I must manipulate to get what I want. Such zombies would see the entire world as something for one to consume. Things are useful, until they aren't. Persons are helpful, until they aren't. Then it is time to move along. After all, there are more things to consume and to conquer.

If we are to counteract this terrifying, utilitarian world, we need to enter the practice of wonder. Sometimes, we do need to stop before the ordinary. Take a moment and think about the gift of the most ordinary objects. Books. Flowers. A bubbling stream. Doors.

Doors, you say? Could you name anything more utilitarian? Doors are put on houses, cars, and other buildings to keep out the cold and creatures both small and large. Don't have a door? Then prepare to deal with mosquitoes, rain, burglars, and bears.

But is this the only reason we have doors? Can our encounter with doors be reduced to that of a "use object"?

Experience testifies otherwise. Wander through a neighborhood and notice the often-bright colors used for doors on houses. The door seems to be calling out, "Come here and enter me, for inside, you are indeed very welcome." Stand before the doors of an important building and notice how impressive the entrance is. Doors often have messages placed upon them, communicating to the one entering the kind of place being passed into. Artists have treated doors as sculptures, testifying to the gravity of what unfolds in a particular building. If you go to Rome, you'll see all sorts of august doors, many that aren't used very often at all. One door is only opened every twenty-five years or so, a Jubilee door that pilgrims use four times per century. To the utilitarian, what a waste! If you opened that door, you could more efficiently move tourists from point A to point B.

But maybe the point of doors isn't efficiency alone but something else. After all, doors are liminal spaces, betwixt and between the outside and the inside. The outside is a space of the unknown, even hostility. Take one walk in South Bend during winter, and you come to recognize how wonderful entering a door is. You go from the windswept, frigid, and snowy outside world into the hearth of your home. Awaiting you is not fear of frostbite or hypothermia but a hot meal and friendly companions to share it all with. To walk through such a door is to move from the aggression of the world to the hospitality of home.

Church doors are a bit different. When you pass through the door of a church, you move from the immensity of the cosmos outside, from the noise of construction and business and traffic, to the silent stillness of worship. The doors of churches are intended as objects to focus us, redirecting our attention from the myriad of "things" in the world to the source of all "meaning" in the world—the living God who has pitched his tent among us.

This transition happens both in grand basilicas in Rome and in small country parishes in Oklahoma. Yes, the experience is a bit different. Walking into St. Peter's Basilica, you come face-to-face with the immensity of what Christ has accomplished upon the Cross. The hectic quality of Rome doesn't entirely disappear, as countless pilgrims advance through the largest church in the world to kneel before the bones of St. Peter (or to take photos to post on Instagram, but that's a story for another day). Yet the grandeur of the space overwhelms, an artistic proclamation that the meaning of redemption is higher, deeper, and far more all-encompassing than our occasionally reductive minds can grasp.

But if you're ever in Harthorne, Oklahoma, the same marvelous transition takes place. At Holy Rosary Catholic Church, you pass from the fields and farmland of rural Oklahoma into the nave of a small country church. The sound of cicadas fades away as you are ushered into the body of the church, looking upon a lit crucifix over an altar. To the side is a small tabernacle where the faithful gather to spend a moment with the Eucharistic Lord, to give thanks and ask God to intercede for all things troubling. Candles flicker, tangible evidence of prayers offered by men and women with whom each of us shares a relationship in Christ's Body, even though we may never know who they are.

You see, doors really do matter. They're part of the instructional wisdom of a church building, one intended to usher us from the world of productivity toward a space of contemplative wonder—to a world suffused with meaning. Look up! The church ceiling decorated like the heavens invites us to look anew at the starry skies outside. Look left and right! The stained-glass windows are not just ways of letting light into a space but a proposal to see how the totality of creation can be transformed in light—natural light as filtered through depictions of Christ's life or the saints in an explosion of playful color.

Every object in a church building, therefore, is significant rather than merely functional. Yes, there are better ways to keep spaces well-lit in the electric age, but a flickering candle isn't about efficiency. Candles, if we are attentive, are strange objects. The light and heat that they provide are given through the self-gift of the wax by which they are made. Their fuel comes from within and not from without. Perhaps this is why, very early on, Christians recognized that the candle is a privileged symbol of Christ. He is the Light of the world, and the source of that light is his very being—the God-man, who loved us to the end (cf. Jn. 13:1). Material candles, one day, run out of fuel. But not Jesus Christ! Ascended into heaven, his love for every human being burns with the fiery intensity of God. See the candle, and recognize the presence of the Beloved who burns with love for you.

Church doors provide this meaningful transition, moving us from a technocratic way of looking at matter as just stuff that we use for our own well-being and comfort to a sacramental one. Material things are bearers of meaning that we do not create but first receive. Through this sacramental way of teaching us to look, we return to the world with vision reformed. The entire cosmos testifies to the presence of the Beloved.

As we move out from the door of the church back into the world at the end of Mass, the task is to take this way of seeing with us. The hungry neighbor on the street is no mere obstacle but the living presence of Christ beckoning us to respond with Eucharistic charity. The created order is not an object for us to use—exclusively for the sake of our own ends—but a gift that once recognized is most appropriately greeted with a hymn of praise.

And if you find yourself moving away from sacramental wonder, don't worry. There's always a church door to pass through, to begin afresh this sacramental way of seeing.

Behold, Believe, Become

1. Think about your own passing through the variety of doors in your life. Your home. Your workplace. What is it like to enter each space? How is entering a church building different from other entrances for you?

2. As you pass through the door of a church building, you discover that everything possesses a meaning grounded in Jesus Christ. What do you typically notice when you enter a church building? How does this material thing bring you toward a deeper understanding of Jesus Christ?

3. You don't always have access to a church door, but you do have access to the practice of wonder! Choose one object or person that you encounter in your life, and compose a short paragraph each day for a month about what this object or person means to you. After doing this for a month, reflect on how this practice has changed the way that you see this object or person.

Scan this code or visit **http://www.avemariapress.com/behold-believe-become-videos** to watch a video from Tim O'Malley and the Bulman family on meeting Christ in thresholds.

3.

THE FONT

Some years ago, I went for a hike with my Boy Scout troop. Despite the apocalyptic predictions of rainfall, our Scoutmaster (not one to be all that anxious about the elements) did not cancel the trip. We started off in the rain. The rain poured down harder. We arrived at the campsite, setting up our tents in the constant rain. We tried to start a fire, but the rain prevailed. We attempted to sleep, but the rain began to seep into our tents. We woke up in the rain. We hiked back in the rain, crossing streams so flushed with water that we needed to construct temporary bridges to ensure safety. At last, we arrived at our cars, and for the first time in over twenty-four hours, our water-logged selves were out of the rain.

It's rare for many of us in the West to be dramatically affected by the cosmic elements. Yes, there is heat. Yes, there are droughts. Yes, there is frigid cold. But we also have air-conditioning, bottled water, and central heating. Natural disasters happen, but they are rare enough that when they do occur, they make a significant impact upon public consciousness. Hurricanes receive round-the-clock coverage because they remind us that human beings are significantly affected by the cosmos—a fact that we mortals who suffer from prideful self-importance have forgotten. If we educate enough civil engineers to build houses on the sides of mountains, then we falsely begin to believe that we possess control over those mountains. But then come the mudslides and wildfires that wipe away our foolish dreams.

What we have forgotten is that we are dependent upon the created order. We are ourselves natural beings immersed in those primordial elements of air, water, earth, and fire. We breathe, and if the air is poisoned, then we die. We drink, and if there is no water, we die. We stand upon the earth, and when it shakes and rocks, so too do our homes. Our temperature is delicate, and we need fire to sustain ourselves.

Our natural dependence should invite us to think differently about the baptismal font, which greets us when we pass through the doors of the church. Water sustains life, but it also drowns us. A beautiful lake on a warm summer day is a source of delight and refreshment, while that same lake experienced in the middle of a cold night is more like a watery abyss. You don't need to be Christian to have such insights; and, in fact, the mythological import of water is shared across most cultures and religions. Water is the most primordial of symbols.

But the genius of Christianity is that the significance of the natural world is taken up into the history of salvation. In the beginning, the world was created out of the watery chaos of nothingness. Water was ordered and controlled by God.

Sin, as we discover in the great flood in Genesis, unleashed the watery chaos anew; only through divine intervention could Noah escape the devastating flood. Israel passed through the Red Sea dry-shod, liberated along the way from their captors. From the Temple in Jerusalem, water flowed forth, giving life to all those who came to worship the God of Abraham, of Isaac, and of Jacob. At the beginning of his ministry, Jesus was baptized in the waters of the Jordan and then sent by the Spirit into the desert, where he thirsted for God alone. All the characteristics of water are discernable: quenching thirst and drowning, giving life and dealing death.

It's no accident that entrance into Christian life involves a descent into the waters of Baptism. Baptism is no quaint rite of passage, a cultural practice for expressing gratitude for a new child. Baptism instead is death and life alike. We die to sin, we live with Christ. Dead to purely natural relationships, and alive to sonship and daughtership in Jesus. Dead to attachment to material things, and alive to the emerging recognition that the only thing which can quench our thirst is God alone. If we try to fill ourselves with other goods, we'll be poisoned. There is a dizzying array of things for us to pursue as we try to quench our thirst—power, money, fame, fortune, booze, revenge, and all the shadowy demons of this age. The whole of Christian life is recognizing our parchedness and drinking from the wellspring that is Christ's own life—one characterized by self-giving love.

And that's what you're pledging to do when you enter the doors of the church, dip your hands into the font, and sign yourself with the Cross of Christ. Just as water drowns, the waters of the font must kill within us all disordered desires. Just as water gives life, we must turn to Christ and drink lustily from the font of his mercy. The very act of dipping our fingers into holy water is a moment of remembering the precarity of this whole project (and, in fact, of our whole existence), how dependent we are not upon our own efforts but on the gratuity of the God who is love. For after dipping our hands into the saving font, we mark our bodies with the Sign of the Cross. In the name of the Father, the Son, and the Holy Spirit. Our whole selves must be ordered to the Cross, to Christ's burning desire for us as he was lifted up on the tree for all to behold. We depend on water, but we depend all the more on the Cross of Christ.

This dependence, in fact, is what every Mass proposes to us. Baptism is not a one-and-done affair. Each time we approach the altar, we exercise our deepest identities as sons and daughters of God. We are called to eat and drink at the Supper of the Lamb. As you immerse your fingers into these life-saving waters, meditate upon what you desire. Do you thirst for God? Do you thirst for something else? And remember that the God who calls you to drink from the wellsprings of life comes to satisfy, at least for a moment in this holy sacrament, the heart that thirsts for him alone: "O taste and see that the LORD is good; happy are those who take refuge in him" (Ps 34:8).

Behold, Believe, Become

1. Make a list of all the natural elements of the cosmos upon which you are dependent. In recognizing how dependent you are upon the cosmos, what new insights do you have about your identity as a creature?

2. Water is a natural element, which has been taken up by God for the sake of salvation. Water kills and gives life; it drowns and it quenches thirst. Thinking upon your own life in Christ, where is there need for death, for something to come to an end? Where do you see a need for new life?

3. The next time you go to Mass, dip your fingers into the font and sign yourself with the Cross. Then sit down. Ask yourself: What are you currently thirsting for? Is it a source of life or death? What would you need to change in order to thirst for God alone? Ask for the grace of such thirst during the celebration of Mass that day.

Scan this code or visit **http://www.avemariapress.com/behold-believe-become-videos** to watch a video from Tim O'Malley and the Bulman family on meeting Christ in water.

4.

PROCESSION

Have you ever paid attention to people walking? Some people move with a certain relaxed rhythm, swinging their arms as they traipse about. Some—especially city dwellers—have an aggressive gait, as if they are preparing at any moment to transition from walking into a fevered run. Time is money, and they're incarnating this piece of productive wisdom in their pace. Lovers, holding hands, seem to be moving as if they have nowhere particular to be. And they don't, because walking next to one's beloved is the whole purpose of the journey to begin with. Small children rarely just walk. They are constantly moving between walking, skipping, jumping, doing cartwheels, and stopping to behold whatever small object has occupied their attention. When my daughter was young, most walks were at least ninety minutes, and they tended to involve no more than a loop around the neighborhood—for there were countless wonders to examine along the way.

The dilemma today is that we may be forgetting a good deal about the art of walking. Go to a college campus and watch the undergraduates. Rather than walk next to another person, engaged in conversation about nothing in particular, their heads are turned downward toward some digital device. Or why walk when it's easier to travel with speed? Why not buy an electric scooter and travel on sidewalks with the sort of haste that threatens the lives of pedestrians (who are also not paying attention, because they are looking at their phones)? I am a fervent walker, the kind who likes to take in seven miles per day. If I can walk somewhere, I will. But it's not unusual for me to encounter friends who stop in their cars while I'm walking, wondering why I would choose to move about in such an unproductive manner. *Tim, do you need a ride? Is everything okay?*

Commuting, though, is only one dimension of walking. Walking tends to reveal something about the interior state of the walker. If you notice someone walking down your street, furtively glancing to and fro, you may wonder what this person is up to. Their very body seems to be expressing something nefarious. The same goes for someone who is nervous, fretting over a particular matter. They pace back and forth as if they are a creature trapped in a cage. We recognize a certain eloquence upon the part of the walker whose head is held high and who possesses an upright posture. Notice that we even refer to virtuous people as upright.

What does it mean that we begin Mass with a processional mode of walking? Walking in a procession is not harried. Heads are held high. There is a controlled quality to the walking, something between a dance and a commute—especially when the procession is accompanied by music. Objects of importance are carried along in the procession, such as a book and a cross. Unusual clothing is worn—chasubles and stoles and miters aplenty.

While Catholics are quite good at these processions, we are not alone. Go to a university commencement and behold the entrance of professors clad in their regalia. See the appearance of the university mace and the platform party who slowly process in. When something is joyfully important, seriously wonderful, we process.

At the start of Mass, we've all entered the church, marked ourselves with holy water, sat, and prayed, but the procession is the beginning of the Mass proper. The ritual walking functions as an invitation to deeper meditation on the meaning of Eucharistic worship. The procession is both playful and serious. Normal fashion and ways of moving are bracketed out. There is the play of beautiful objects and clothing alike. But importantly, the liturgical actors maintain a certain seriousness of both expression and gait. The liturgy is not a farce but the efficacious work of God, who still acts among us here and now. It is a playful seriousness, a serious playfulness.

In London, I once saw a boys' choir process into Westminster Cathedral at the beginning of an evening daily Mass. They were dressed in the sort of cassocks that you would expect a British boys' choir to wear. Their hair was also tussled, presumably because this final Mass was the conclusion of a day involving not only singing but sports and running and other activities that define the lives of young boys. Their faces were serious, but you could not help but perceive a mischievous twinkle in the eye. Asked to turn on a dime as they reached the sanctuary of the church, not a few stumbled as they made the pivot. As an observer to the whole affair, I found myself ever more confident that such playful serious-ness is precisely the right disposition to take up before the living God.

And in the end, that's the ultimate meaning of the pro-cession. We are not just taking a walk, giving people a bit of extra time to get into their seats before the liturgical act commences. Rather, we are walking *toward the altar of God!*

This orientation is the fundamental disposition of the Christian life. Christian existence is not the lackadaisical meandering of a couple in love, who have nowhere in partic-ular to be. Ours is a movement *toward* God. Every human life is a procession, with fits and starts along the way. We begin in life, we end in death, and things happen in between. But the procession of a Christian has a distinctive orientation—toward union with the triune God.

It doesn't matter during the week between Masses if you haven't made much progress. On Sunday morning, it's time to start the procession anew, to be reordered once more to one's ultimate destiny. It's a serious affair, this Christian wor-ship. Not because the purpose of the whole thing is to have majestic preaching and singing. If that's your interest, go to the concert hall where it will likely be both more professional and more beautiful. No, the serious quality of our worship is that we are moving toward the God who made the first move toward us, the One who is still moving toward us, meeting us along the way.

So as the procession begins, recognize the serious and playful drama that is to unfold on the altar. The great procession of God into the world unfolds among us once more. The God who created the world, who walked among us, who took flesh, who died upon the Cross and rose again, who ascended into heaven, and who sent the Spirit into the world now comes to accompany us anew.

Get up and greet this God who is once more on the move. Let your disposition be both serious and playful at once. Delight in the playful music and the beautiful colors. But as you rejoice, do so as one who remembers why we're processing in the first place. Once upon a time, our ancestors turned away from God. This very week, each of us has turned away from God. But the very good news is that we get to start off again, to turn toward the Lord who is our destiny.

Behold, Believe, Become

1. Reflect on the quality of your own walking. How would you characterize it? What does it reveal about your own relationship with time?

2. The procession is a reorientation toward Christ, moving toward the God who is our ultimate destiny. Where in your life are you moving in the right direction? Where do you need to return to the Lord?

3. Go for a walk one day around your neighborhood, praying the Rosary along the way. Afterward, think about how the act of praying changed the way that you walked. What might you take from this practice into your own way of walking in the context of the Mass?

Scan this code or visit **http://www.avemariapress.com/behold-believe-become-videos** to watch a video from Tim O'Malley and the Bulman family on meeting Christ in movement.

5.

THE BODY
AND THE CROSS

Critiques of Catholic worship generally go something like this: Catholics mindlessly repeat the same motions and words without proper understanding. Ritual, in this case, replaces what should be worship in spirit and in truth. That is sincere worship. A Catholic goes to Mass, and then they think they have worshipped God by kneeling and standing and saying words they say every week. Sincere worship, on the other hand, demands that we first have the desire to worship and then choose the proper form by which that desire is expressed. If someone is full of joy, why would they kneel? If they want to express sorrow before God, why would they sing an Easter hymn of praise?

With all critiques, there is something to listen to here. Yes, there is a form of worship in which we believe that our ritual acts placate God. If we go to Mass and do the right things, then we have fulfilled our obligation before God (even if and especially when we didn't want to worship God in the first place). Today, one might call this cultural

Catholicism—a sense that checking some ritual box is sufficient for the performance of one's Catholic identity. *Listen, I
go to Mass on Easter and Christmas. My kids have received the
sacraments. Must I really understand such actions as occasions
of prayer, of communion with the triune God? I have, after all,
fulfilled my obligations.*

Contrary to the objections of the cultural Catholic, it is
important to engage in the liturgical act with understanding
that involves our full selves—our memory, our imaginations,
our understanding, and our wills. We should not only go to
Mass but want to participate fully in the mystery of divine
love. We want to become holy.

But let's not too quickly move away from the focus of
this meditation—the use of the body in the act of worship.
The presumption that prescribed ritual action is insincere
is deficient. For example, some see making the Sign of the
Cross as an empty gesture. But this presumption about ritual
action tends to operate out of a faulty understanding of what
it means to be a human being—namely, that we are nothing
more than minds in bodies, and what really matters is the
mind. The mind comes to the decision to worship God. The
body then will react from this understanding. We *feel*
like worshipping God, and then we choose the form that
we think best conforms to our affections. It's the kind of
decision that leads one to wonder, *Why do I have to worship
God at Mass? Can't I take a walk in a field and experience the
same presence of God?*

Happily, this is not who human beings are. Our bodies enable us to express the deepest dimensions of our souls and what ultimately matters to us. Think about hugging your child. You don't first think to yourself, "I love this creature, and therefore I ought to enact this through some physical act. Let me choose a hug." No! You simply hug your child, embracing your beloved son or daughter. Such hugging is not the result of some prior act of thinking. Rather, as you hug, you learn to love your child all the more. You write upon your body a habit of loving.

Let's think about this in relation to the Sign of the Cross. That's where every Mass starts. You place your fingers upon your head, move down your chest, then toward your left shoulder, and then to the right one. This act shouldn't be done quickly. In this moment of contemplative action, you are acknowledging that all of your prayer begins with this particular body, which has been baptized into the name of the Father, the Son, and the Holy Spirit. Everything that happens for the rest of Mass depends on this redeemed sack of flesh and bones. And dear me, the more you do this Sign of the Cross, the more you remember it.

We think about memory exclusively as a mental act. *I remember this math equation. I remember this story and can recall it. I remember in my mind—that's where memory does its work.* But our bodies remember too. I was raised in East Tennessee right in the heart of the Smoky Mountains. The moment I arrive back in Knoxville, Tennessee, I feel at once

at home. The sound of bluegrass and Rocky Top on a Saturday afternoon. The scent of dogwood trees, honeysuckle, and
barbecue. The sight of those blue-gray foothills clothed in
smoke. The taste of moonshine, tomatoes, and sweet potato
pie. The texture of root-covered hiking trails. This is East
Tennessee. And with every physical act while I'm there, I
remember more what it means to dwell there. I long for it
even more.

Think about the number of Masses you might have
been to. How many times have you marked your body with
the Sign of the Cross? To begin this motion, as you have
done countless times before, is to arrive at home. That Mass
you went to after you heard your grandmother was dying.
Your wedding Mass. The funeral Mass of the young man or
woman whom you loved and who ended his or her own life.
The ordinary Sunday Mass. At each one, you began in the
name of the Father, the Son, and the Holy Spirit.

Sometimes, we think about religious practice as something dramatic. You have to cry or raise your hands in praise
or make a fundamental decision that will change the rest of
your life. Of course, those things happen. And what a gift
they are! But they are not the ordinary way we praise God.
The ordinary way is the daily, consistent, loving commitment
to the triune God. And that involves our bodies.

When I go to Mass and make the Sign of the Cross, I
do so intentionally, slowly, recollecting what I am saying.
What makes my prayer possible is not my peculiar spiritual

genius. Rather, it is because I have plunged myself into the God who is Father, Son, and Holy Spirit. That's where prayer begins. It begins with the recognition that God is gift. Our bodies at Baptism were immersed into that Love that happily shatters our rather limited capacity for love. And in the years since, we have marked our bodies again and again with that mystery of love. It doesn't matter if we have not always deserved it (who has?). It doesn't matter if we have not always understood what we're doing (who does?). It doesn't matter if we have not always wanted to (who would?). In the name of the Father, the Son, and the Holy Spirit.

At every Mass, we start afresh. Not because we have advanced in our cognitive grasping of God. Not because we have earned some new status that we previously did not possess. But because we begin again by signing this sack of flesh and bones, this now glorious body redeemed by Jesus Christ through the waters of Baptism. In the name of the Father, the Son, and the Holy Spirit. May each of us live up to that remarkable identity.

Behold, Believe, Become

1. Think about the countless times that you have signed yourself in the name of the Father, the Son, and the Holy Spirit. What has this bodily act meant to you? When

you make the Sign of the Cross outside of Mass, what happens?

2. What does it mean to you that worship involves our bodies? How have you encountered Jesus Christ in this worship that involves your body?

3. As you pass a church building or chapel in your town (maybe go out of your way to do so), make the Sign of the Cross. How does this change the way that you commute? How does this act come with you into the regular celebration of the Eucharist?

Scan this code or visit **http://www.avemariapress.com/behold-believe-become-videos** to watch a video from Tim O'Malley and the Bulman family on meeting Christ with our bodies.

6.

THE NAVE

Human children are precarious creatures. A foal is born, able to walk mere hours after birth. Puppies, requiring more assistance than young horses, can function apart from their parents within eight weeks. Human children, on the other hand, need adults to care for them in a committed manner for the first decade or so of their lives. And this care does not cease once they are able to procure food or take care of basic needs. Human beings need one another throughout their lives for friendship and companionship. We are social animals.

One of the marks of the modern social order is a forgetfulness of our vocation toward companionship. We have traded our dependence upon one another for a raw, naked individualism. The driver who refuses to ask for directions, lest he appear incompetent. The student who will not ask for assistance from her professor, believing that she can do it by herself. The young man or woman who seeks to demand nothing of his or her partner, lest they appear too needy, too dependent upon another person for happiness. The displacement of the elderly and those with special needs from our communities, because their dependency asks too much from those of us who have imagined that we are nondependent creatures. This myth of the individual, going it alone no matter the cost, is surely one of the roots of the epidemic of loneliness that plagues us today.

The opposite myth, though, has been similarly present in modernity. Here, the individual disappears, swallowed up by the collectivity. Think about totalitarian regimes or even the kind of social pressure that operates in certain suburban neighborhoods—if you're going to be happy, then you have to possess the kind of life that we believe is the right one. There is nothing except the collective entity, and for this reason, the individual disappears. Conscience departs. The interior life is assaulted, reshaped by the propaganda of the society. Give yourself over to the collective mass, or pay the consequence.

Sometimes in life, the goal is to find the happy mean. Maybe we just need a bit of collectivity and a bit of individuality, and we'll get the formula right—avoiding both the loneliness caused by individualism and the social misery enacted by totalitarianism. But two falsehoods do not generally combine to make a right. Instead, we need a proper understanding of the relationship between the collective and the individual.

Such an understanding can be found in the very identity of what it means to be an individual person. Each one of us is a particular person, who has never existed before. The things that have formed me to think a certain way about the world have not formed you, and vice versa. We may possess certain universals in common—that is, we are born, and we die. But I have been shaped by what has happened to me, and so have you. When I encounter you, therefore, I am encountering an unknown person—and not just because I don't know your name. Rather, you are a mystery to me. You will always remain a mystery to me because you're not an object in the world that I can master. You are a person whose story is not my own, with whom I am called to relate rather than control.

Now we have the basis of a community. Community life isn't about erasing our identities, pretending that we are all the same. Instead, community life is grounded in a common commitment of various persons who are mysteries unto themselves and to one another. I need you to better understand who I am. You need me. We need each other. Relationality does not erase individuality but allows us to become individual persons who undertake a process of both self and mutual understanding in a community. We become more ourselves when we are in relationship with others.

Christianity finds the root of this mystery in the very identity of God as triune—Father, Son, and Holy Spirit. God is three persons and one essence. Personhood in God is fundamentally relational. It can't be at the level of essence (what something ultimately is), because then there would be three gods: a Father-God, a Son-God, a Spirit-God. Instead, the terms are relational. The Father is who he is because he is the Father of the Son. The Son is the Son of the Father. The

Spirit is the love of the Father and the Son. God is known in unity, but a unity that is relational.

Divine unity, therefore, doesn't erase distinctions. Erasing distinctions is what happens in a totalitarian society: if you are to belong to this or that political body, then you have to give up who you are. Yet at the same time, in God there is not pure chaos, just a bunch of individuals competing with one another for power and prestige. Instead, in true unity, there is difference.

What does it mean that we are created in the image and likeness of God? We, too, are ordered toward a unity that does not erase difference. We don't look like God, because God doesn't have a body. But we are made for self-gift, for belonging to one another. We belong to God, and therefore we belong to one another.

After all, isn't this what we do at every Mass when we assemble in the nave to worship God? The word *nave* comes from the Latin word for "ship." It's where the faithful gather to worship God in the church building. In both ancient and medieval Christianity, the nave wasn't quite the organized space it is today. All the people came inside the church building to worship Jesus Christ together. They did not leave behind their identity, but their common act of worship united them together. It didn't matter if one was the emperor or a poor man (although, the emperor did tend to have a much more pleasant seat). They belonged to one another.

So, when you gather in the nave of the Church to encounter Jesus Christ at every Mass, you are realizing something essential to your identity as a creature. You need other Christians for the act of worship. You are dependent upon others. You give yourself over to the rites of the Church, trying to attune your voice to your neighbor in the act of worship. The goal is not to be the true worshipper of God, the one who has far more devotion than those seated to your left and right. Instead, you say the words that you're supposed to. You sing what you're supposed to. You do so not in a way that draws attention to yourself but as a way of joining in offering one voice of praise to the triune God.

But let's remember that, in the act of worship, your individuality is not erased. As you practice this unity in worship, you remain a person distinct from all those you are gathering with. You come into the Mass as one who has experienced the joy of a new marriage or the sorrow of a spousal death. No one else has your exact story. And yet, we can all worship together. We worship together because each of our stories requires the stories of others to be complete.

In this sense, we are like the stones that make up a building (an image that the First Letter of Peter draws upon). If you look upon a building, every stone is different. But the building depends upon each of these stones working in concert with one another. True harmony requires distinction after all.

You have probably noticed how images of the saints are often found in the main body or nave of churches. This is no accident. After all, what is a saint? A saint is a member of a community that precedes him or her. A saint has conformed himself or herself to the mystery of Christ, because he or she is part of the city of God who praises the triune God for eternity. But that common identity as a saint does not erase the particularities. St. Augustine, St. Thérèse of Lisieux, and St. Teresa Benedicta of the Cross are all individuals with particular life stories. Heaven doesn't erase that particularity. It doesn't erase the charisms or particular gifts of the Spirit that the saints have received. But those charisms are now taken up in a bigger story, a gathering of the common worship of all the angels and the saints.

The nave, therefore, is the place where the faithful, the whole assembly, learn to be citizens of the Communion of Saints. We individuals need one another. We need everyone who is there, everyone who is baptized into Christ's Body: the intellectually disabled, the poor man or woman, the out-of-tune cantor, the wealthy business person, the child in the womb, the teenager struggling to recognize the presence of God, the migrant, and the uber-committed parishioner who participates in every Bible study. In the nave, you'll find them all.

The Church does not demand that individual particularity be erased. After all, it's not the Church's ministers who have gathered us for this act of worship. The Church is not some sort of club that has generated an interesting collection of rules for membership. This is Christ's sacrificial work, his invitation to woo every man and woman into a communion of love that transcends anything that we can create.

Therefore, as we gather at Mass, bring your whole self. Enter the nave aware of the concrete lives of so many individuals, seeking to worship the living God. But also ask that the Spirit can unite us into a greater unity, into a common voice of praise that is a foretaste of heaven itself. And in conducting this grand experiment (one set into motion by God), we will leave that church building far more capable of letting this little bit of heaven spill over into every relationship we have.

Behold, Believe, Become

1. This meditation identified two temptations of modern life: we suffer from either extreme individualism or a totalitarian sense of community that erases difference. Where have you experienced one or both of these temptations?

2. In the nave, we gather as persons worshipping God with one another. What might you have to learn from this common worship that does not erase individuality? What might you have to learn from your fellow Catholics?

3. Do a bit of research on saints whom you admire. Notice what makes each one different, what their particular gifts

are. Reflect on your own gifts, and perhaps ask other people what they think your gift is. The next time that you go to Mass, think about this gift, offering it to God during the Eucharistic Prayer.

Scan this code or visit **http://www.avemariapress.com/behold-believe-become-videos** to watch a video from Tim O'Malley and the Bulman family on meeting Christ in gathering spaces.

7.

WORDS

We don't usually think about words as material objects, do we? Words—like the sentences found in a textbook—are intended to communicate ideas. If the word is spoken, then it's fleeting, disappearing as soon as we have spoken it. If the word is written, there's a bit more stability; the word is etched upon a page. But the goal of the etching is to communicate thoughts from one person to another. When I leave a note for my spouse, "I'll be home at six," I am telling my wife something. The materiality of the note matters less than the communication of information.

But not all words are like this, are they? Sometimes, words also do something. If I utter a vow, I am not merely communicating a piece of information. No, I am performing an act through words: *I promise that I will be there for your theater performance next Friday. I pledge to uphold this oath of office. I love you and will do so forever, even when it's difficult.* Such words have consequences. With increasing commitment, they involve my whole body, my full self, in the utterance of such words. *I will be there on Friday in the flesh. I will commit myself to the common good of the political order. I give my whole self to you.*

Furthermore, words also have a materiality that common usage makes us forget. Think for a moment about the words *heavy* and *light*. Say them aloud. Notice that the word *heavy* sounds a bit like what it means. The final syllable drops down. *Light*, in contrast, elevates. The single syllable flows out of your mouth, seemingly lifting you up in the act of utterance.

To participate fruitfully in the Mass, we must remember that words are both material and performative alike. When we sing the Sanctus, we are not merely communicating information: God is holy, and we're singing this song to express that holiness. No! We are placing ourselves through our speech before the very holiness of God. *Sanctus, sanctus, sanctus.* Holy, holy, holy. *Santo, santo, santo.* God is the source of all holiness, so holy that a single use of the word *holy* is insufficient for the act of praise. This is why the prophet Isaiah himself spoke of God's threefold holiness as he began his prophetic career (Is 6:3). Now, we stand in Isaiah's place immediately before the Eucharistic liturgy, acknowledging that God is *holy, holy, holy.*

As we speak or chant these words, we enter into the presence of that holiness. We don't first have thoughts in our minds about divine holiness, only later uttering the words. *You know what? God must be holy, don't you think? If I pour over the pages of scripture, God's glory is obvious on every page.*

What might be the best way to express this? I know, I will say, "Holy, holy, holy," three times. I have done so.

Instead, the words do the work for us. They bring us into the presence of divine holiness; they give us the speech to express contrition for our sins and to confess our faith in God's power in our lives. *Glory to God in the highest. I confess to almighty God. I believe in one God. . . .*

On the other hand, the words aren't magic. You can, after all, make a promise that you won't keep. *I will love you forever, unless it gets too hard. I will keep my oath of office, unless the right bribe comes along. I really wanted to go to your theater performance, but then something much better came along. Alas.*

Participation in the Mass does require that we attune our mind to our voices, that we understand not only the literal meaning of the words that we listen to, utter, or sing but also the consequences of these words for our lives. When we hear our Lord in the gospels telling us to forgive seventy-seven times, this is no pious sentiment. If we are to listen to these words properly, then our act of listening must change us. Do we take our Lord at his word? Do we let our interior and exterior words (what we think, what we say, and how we act) be transformed because of what we have heard at Mass?

This is why the words spoken at Mass must be said in a way that is not too fast, nor too plodding. The goal is a sort of contemplative understanding, letting ourselves become more wholly attuned to what we speak or sing. It is akin to the speech of a lover, who delightfully attends to every word that comes forth from the mouth of his beloved. It is like listening to the words of a poem, where it is not enough to understand the literal "meaning" of the words but necessary also to take up the deeper "sense" that the poet is communicating through the words.

Such full, conscious, and active participation in speaking, singing, and listening to the words of the Mass finds its icon in the Blessed Virgin Mary. Medieval altarpieces often placed in the central panel the Annunciation, the moment in which the angel of the Lord informed Mary of her unique role in salvation history. Such imagery tended to include the Virgin Mother reading a book just as the angel arrived. Before the Word became flesh in her womb, she had been contemplating the Word of God in sacred scripture. In her dialogue with the angel Gabriel, she speaks words informed by her contemplation of the sacred page. She has attuned herself to God's will; therefore, she is able to say: "Let it be with me according to your word" (Lk 1:38). *Let the Spirit descend upon me, let me have my part in salvation history, and let me bear within my womb the Word made flesh.*

The words of the Blessed Virgin, certainly, have had material and consequential weight for the history of the world. They were not just an act of communication but a performative gift of self. The stunning thing is that, at every Mass, the same drama of salvation is made available to us who let our minds and hearts be attuned to what we speak, say, or listen to. We will not give birth to Jesus in the flesh, but we do possess a "womb of the heart" in which Christ's Word can take flesh anew. The divine Word can dwell among us in the furnace of our heart's desire.

So, we should indeed understand what is being spoken or sung at every Mass. Such understanding isn't akin to mastery, getting so good at every jot and tittle of the Mass texts and chants that we no longer need to think about them. The more that we understand, the more there is to ponder in these weighty words. Such pondering gives space for the Holy Spirit to overshadow us, letting Christ's presence come anew into our hearts.

Behold, Believe, Become

1. When have you spoken or heard words that felt especially weighty, leading not only to information communicated but to a very sharing of one's self? What were the words? If these words were spoken some time ago, what do they mean to you now?

2. What words at Mass are especially attractive to you? Which ones do you struggle to understand (either their literal meaning or their deeper sense)? What words at Mass do you need to become flesh in your life right now?

3. In the quiet preceding the beginning of the Mass, repeat to yourself at least ten times the words spoken by the Virgin Mary at the Annunciation: "Let it be with me

according to your word" (Lk 1:38). Do so in a way that
is neither plodding nor speedy. Pay attention after Mass:
How has this practice enabled you to participate better
in speaking, listening to, and singing the words of the
Mass?

Scan this code or visit **http://www.avemariapress.com/behold-
believe-become-videos** to watch a video from Tim O'Malley and
the Bulman family on meeting Christ in spoken words.

8.

BREAD AND WINE

If you're addicted to speed and efficiency, baking bread is probably not for you. It takes time and a bit of patience. If you're too sloppy with mixing ingredients for the dough, the whole thing goes awry. Too impatient while waiting for the dough to rise? Good luck having bread that is remotely edible. Rushing in to put the bread into the oven? You'll likely be consuming half-baked dough rather than proper bread.

Making wine is likewise a time-intensive procedure. Grapes are to be grown and harvested. They are to be crushed, then left to ferment. You bottle that wine, and the longer you wait (usually), the better the vintage becomes.

For the most part, those of us schooled in the haste of modernity are not experts at such waiting. We want things right now. Instant meals. Instant shopping. Instant answers to all the questions that puzzle us. "Now" has almost become too late.

Such natural staples as bread and wine prophetically speak out against the addiction to speed. Bread is better if we take more time with it. Wine is worth more if you don't gulp it down all at once the moment alcohol has made an appearance in the mixture.

Early Christians, such as St. Augustine, saw in the use of bread and wine at Mass an image of the slowness of conversion. Attuning yourself to the mystery of Christ takes time. Bread comes about by growing wheat, harvesting it, pounding it down, baking it, and then serving it. Wine has the same unhurried agricultural process; the same almost-violent process of conversion is required. Bread and wine are created through a gradual application of force. To Augustine, that process is akin to what it takes to become a Christian.

This understanding of Christian identity is discordant with how many Americans approach life in Christ. Conversion is understood as an instantaneous process. Once you were in sin; now you're not. Once you were in darkness, now only light. Once you were; now you are and ever shall be, world without end. Amen.

But what if real conversion is a far more time-intensive process than the immediacy of an altar call or a single experience in one's youth? The best things in human life, after all, take time. You fall in love with your spouse, but then ideally you spend the rest of your existence deepening this love. You become an expert in some craft or art, but as you exercise this expertise, you recognize how much further you have to go. The more you learn, the more you discover that you don't know.

The signs of bread and wine are material invitations to come to terms with the long-term transformation required of disciples. After all, what happens to those elements of bread and wine that are placed on the altar? They are transformed, becoming the Body and Blood of Christ through the words spoken by the priest. These words are not his own creation but those given to us by Jesus himself: *This is my body, given for you. This is my blood, poured out for you. Do this in memory of me.*

Yes, the transformation of those gifts takes place at once. Words are spoken, and elements are transformed. They are no longer bread and wine; instead they are the personal presence of our Lord given to us under the signs of bread and wine. Here is our Lord! It's why we pause in wondrous silence before these Eucharistic elements. It's why we bow with reverence before we receive these elements. Our Lord has come to dwell among us.

Nonetheless, our perception fails to see this. We don't see the Lord made present upon the altar, but we see only the signs of bread and wine. Yes, on the altar, it is no longer bread and wine at the level of substance or being. It is Christ. We see him. But the signs are the only things there for us to behold. It may be the Body of Christ, but the Eucharistic element of bread can still be fractured. It may be the Blood of Christ dwelling among us, but the sign of wine can still be poured out.

There's something marvelous about our Lord using these elements as the preeminent signs of his personal presence. For the signs of bread and wine reveal that Christ's Eucharistic presence means also a lifetime task of letting ourselves be reshaped by the self-giving love of the Eucharistic Lord. It's not enough to be overwhelmed by his presence for a half hour. We must let our very existence become like the bread that is offered on the altar, broken and fractured to feed the many. We must let our lives become like wine, poured out for the communion of all men and women. This process is truly an extended one, encompassing the totality of our lives. Eucharistic amazement cannot be reduced to mastering a specific doctrine or two related to presence or sacrifice. The self must be attuned to the same time-intensive, sometimes painful process of conversion that makes bread and wine fitting elements for Christ's Eucharistic gift of himself.

Such a transformation takes time. You don't become excellent at Eucharistic self-giving after watching a video evangelist or participating in a six-week small-group study dedicated to the Eucharist. You learn to imitate the self-giving love of Christ through a regular dying to self, attuning yourself to the sacrifice of Christ that is remembered and made present upon the altar every day.

As our days pass, we will discover endless opportunities to let ourselves become ever more like the signs of bread and wine that have themselves become entirely the Body and Blood of Christ. The process will take a while. It will often be painful, as we let the Spirit reshape and rewrite the narrative of our broken selves. The transformation of ourselves into disciples will only be finished, in fact, at our deaths. But until then, we have before us those extraordinary signs of bread and wine, the presence of our Lord given to us, to school us in the art of self-giving love—an art that takes time.

Behold, Believe, Become

1. The modern age moves fast, something we know all too well. What is something that you have learned in your life that took a bit of time? A relationship that took months or years to come to fruition? A slow development of a particular virtue? How did time function as a gift in such situations?

2. In the Eucharist, the bread and wine become the Body and Blood of Christ, while the signs of bread and wine remain for us to contemplate. What do you think you have to learn from these signs of bread and wine about the life of discipleship? Where can you be fractured or poured out for the life of the world?

3. Get together with someone and bake a loaf of bread. Pay attention to the various steps along the way in making this bread. What insights do you have after baking this bread relative to life as a disciple of Jesus Christ? How

might this baking of bread change the way that you think about the Eucharistic elements?

Scan this code or visit **http://www.avemariapress.com/behold-believe-become-videos** to watch a video from Tim O'Malley and the Bulman family on meeting Christ in bread and wine.

9.

THE ALTAR

If you were unfamiliar with Catholic ritual practice, and you entered a parish church, you might be horrified. Such horror would not be precipitated by bad music or dreadful preaching (though I've heard that exists now and again). Instead, at the front of the church is an altar. And typically altars are places for sacrifice. For offering things. For killing creatures. Sometimes, those altars were even used for the sacrifice of human beings.

In the twentieth century, there had been a tendency in Catholicism to tone down this potentially bewildering aspect of the Church's worship. We began to construct the altar more as a table, a place of hospitality, where we dine with the living God and one another. Yes, there's a sacrifice happening here, but more fundamentally, we are gathering to eat a meal. Nothing to see here, just a bunch of Christians dining in the kingdom of God.

This aspect of eating and drinking is integral to the Mass (and will be addressed in a later meditation). But for now, let's attend to the altar as a place of sacrifice. For here we remember something fundamental about what it means to be a human being—we are creatures that possess an extraordinary capacity for love but also a terrifying potential for violence.

We moderns, of course, imagine that we are a post-sacrificial people. Yes, maybe our ancestors used to offer human beings to the gods. That's how they tried to bring about peace in the cosmos. But that was before we all became quite proper and civilized. All it took was a bit of education, and we figured out that peace can be achieved through good will (and a can-do attitude) on our part.

Now, the problem with such a narrative is that it ignores that human beings remain inexorably connected to our animal selves. Yes, we generally no longer slaughter human beings in the public square as a way of appeasing the gods. But we do find a way to turn someone into a scapegoat on social media, seeking to eliminate them from the human community. We manufacture in our minds "others" who are at fault for all the ills of the social body. The immigrant. The foreigner. The person of a different race. The politician (or even ecclesial leader) we despise. It's their fault, their fault, their most grievous fault.

The naivety of the modern age is that we have forgotten the violence that lurks in the hidden places of the human heart. For this reason, sacrifice has migrated from primitive stone altars to the gossipy text messages of neighbors; to the political order where we must find a scapegoat to blame for all social and cultural ills; to the racism and fear of the

neighbor that may surface at any momen
acts of violence.

The purpose of recognizing our prope
ing sacrifice is not to deny the possibility of improvement.
Instead, it is simply to note that we do possess a violent
streak in us as mortal creatures. In confessing this fact, we are
like an alcoholic who has come to terms with the problem
he possesses. He is not saying that he can't get better when
he tells his neighbor that he has a drinking problem. He is
instead saying that getting better requires him to be truthful
about the actual problem.

Hence, the Eucharistic altar. Upon that altar, bread and
wine are offered to the Father through the Son in the unity
of the Holy Spirit. This offering is a sign that makes present
Jesus Christ's own sacrifice of love. Jesus, the God-man, lived
with the consequences of our own sacrificial logic. He was
the scapegoat. He was beaten. He suffered. And he died as
a sacrifice.

And yet, his death was undertaken as an act of love. He
was no normal victim, for he was also a priest. He offered
his life, as the Son, as a fragrant sacrifice to the Father. It was
not the violence that the Father wanted. It was the love, the
willingness to no longer abide in the sacrificial logic that is
the source of our bloodlust. Your neighbor slaps your cheek.
Give him the other. People hate you, blaming everything
upon you. Forgive them. They want to arrest you, shame

you, beat you, whip you, strip you, hate you, slaughter you. *Love them to the end.*

That's the sacrifice of the God-man, Jesus Christ. It is love and love unto the end that descends into the darkest crevices of the human heart. The sacrifice was accepted by the Father, who raised the Son up through the power of the Holy Spirit. *You think you can kill Love made flesh? Well, here Love is raised up. Jesus Christ, the Son of the Father, raised up through the power of the Spirit.* And into every future moment of hatred and violence that you can concoct (and, oh, can you concoct them), his sacrifice of love is intended to offer another way.

The altar at Mass is where this sacrifice is made present. It happens anew, not as some endless reenactment of the gods. It happens anew because Christ is ascended into heaven. He is at the right hand of the Father, and through the signs of bread and wine, he makes his once-and-for-all sacrificial love available to us.

That's why the presence of a stony altar rather than a polished (and pretty) table really matters. The event that unfolds in our parishes is not a dainty meal celebrated for the prim and proper. The Eucharist is Christ's sacrifice. It is the sacrifice that invites us, if we're attentive, to think about a new medicine for our sacrificial malaise. Instead of imagining that we can escape this propensity through a bit of education and good cheer, we need a sobering dose of honesty. The way out of sacrificial logic is through letting our lives become a sacrifice of love.

You want to blame your neighbor for everything terrible that has happened? Tame your anger. You find yourself perturbed by politicians whose connection with the truth is, well, complicated? Pray for them. You need a scapegoat to blame? Love one another.

All of this is easier said than done, huh? But that's also the point of the altar. We as the Church are not gathering around a series of ethical or moral principles, which we hope to pass on to future ages. We are gathered around the sacrifice of the God-man, who brings all men and women to himself. The efficacy of the sacrifice—the way it heals us of our own faulty logic of sacrifice—is not our work alone. It is the work of the Eucharistic Lord, who invites us week after week to the Supper of the Lamb.

Just as the craggy stone of the altar rises up in the sanctuary, becoming a table where the unbloody sacrifice of bread and wine are offered, so too are our stony hearts renewed through the Eucharistic mystery so they can become a sacrificial offering. We trade the violence of sacrifice, of blame, for a Eucharistic hospitality that welcomes all to the altar of God. That's why the priest kisses the altar at the beginning of Mass. It's why we reverence the altar. For in this shaped piece of stone, the salvation of the world is at hand. And as sacrificial addicts, that's good news, indeed.

Behold, Believe, Become

1. Where do you see a tendency in the wider social order for violent sacrifice? How about within you?

2. The altar is a place that provides for us mortal creatures an alternative proposal regarding sacrifice. Through the sacrifice of Christ, we learn the sacrifice of love unto the end. How might this Eucharistic sacrifice help us as a Church, as a society, and as individuals to love one another?

3. Spend a bit of time either before Mass or outside of Mass praying before the altar. Consider people whom you need to love more, whom you are tempted to treat as scapegoats in your life. Be as honest as possible. During Mass, especially during the Eucharistic Prayer, ask Jesus to open up a space for you to love your neighbor in the same way that Christ loved all of us in his sacrifice. Do this for as long as you need to in order to love your neighbor rightly.

Scan this code or visit **http://www.avemariapress.com/behold-believe-become-videos** to watch a video from Tim O'Malley and the Bulman family on meeting Christ in sacrifice.

10.

KNEELING, STANDING, AND SITTING

When we contemplated the act of signing oneself with the Cross, we also attended to the importance of the body in the act of worship. What we do with our bodies is not ancillary to prayer but integral to it. Prayer always involves certain embodied gestures that prepare us to enter into the presence of God. We close our eyes. We open up a book and tenderly caress the pages as we search for our favorite psalm. We breathe in and out, transitioning to mindful recollection before the Lord.

In the Mass, three primary postures are kneeling, sitting, and standing. Each of these postures disposes our bodies to participate fully in the Mass. Reflecting upon these postures can therefore be as fruitful as meditating on the words of the Eucharistic Prayer.

There are very few places outside church buildings in modernity where we kneel or genuflect. I can think of two.

The first is when we are speaking to a young child. Instead of trying to speak to the young child while our posture is upright, we bend down upon a knee to communicate with the child. The second is during a proposal for marriage. Typically, the man drops to one knee in asking for a lifetime commitment to his beloved. Otherwise, we don't regularly kneel in front of persons or objects.

But in the church, there is a good deal of kneeling and bending the knee. We genuflect, crossing ourselves when we enter a pew. We kneel in quiet prayer before Mass starts. During the Eucharistic Prayer, we kneel in adoration before the mystery of Christ's self-giving love made present upon the altar. After Mass, we may return to this posture of kneeling once more, to give thanks for the fruits of this Mass.

Yes, kneeling may be understood as adopting a certain awestruck posture before the transcendent God. God is so full of glory, so wonderful, that there is no option but to pledge ourselves to God. Overcome with wonder, what can we do but bend the knee?

But there's something less obvious about the act of kneeling. Remember that kneeling takes place in moments of vulnerability. We lower ourselves when we speak to the child. We genuflect as we propose to our beloved. In both cases, the act of kneeling down is a moment of self-emptying.

When we kneel, therefore, in the church, we are emptying ourselves. Kneeling is an enactment of humility, a recognition that we are creatures who are worshipping the God who first loved us. In that sense, kneeling is an imitation of God's own bending down in love in the Incarnation. Humility is not hatred of self but is rather an expression of honest love, a desire to be with, and a willingness to make ourselves vulnerable to the person before us. Therefore, as we kneel in the Eucharistic Prayer, we are enacting the very humility, the self-emptying love, that will be required to participate fruitfully in the prayer itself. As we kneel, it's almost as if we are saying with our bodies, "God, take everything. Transform me into a creature who gives everything to you. You were the one who first bent down in love, and may I now do the same."

Based on this discussion of kneeling, you might imagine that standing is therefore a posture of total equality, perhaps even bordering on hubris. We stand before God because we don't possess the proper humility to bend the knee.

In fact, this is not how Christians have traditionally understood standing. In certain places in the early Church, kneeling was not allowed during the season of Easter. This was not because Christians imagined that they were equal to God. Rather, to stand was to recognize how our Baptism into Jesus Christ has fundamentally changed who we are. We are creatures who can stand upright before God because of what Jesus Christ has done for us. We are creatures who can stand with hope because of Jesus. After all, sin had turned us inward (in Latin, *curvatus se*—we were turned in upon ourselves). Our horizon was no longer God but ourselves.

Now, because of Jesus's act of salvation, we can stand upright and look up toward God.

In standing, we announce the glory of the Resurrection with our bodies. We stand when we listen to the Gospel because there the voice of the Lord comes to speak again. We often stand in processions, with eyes ahead, aware of the hope that draws us toward the altar of God. We are like the prodigal or lost son in the Gospel of Luke who has been greeted with infinite mercy by his father. We threw everything away, and although God knows this, God has picked us up.

So, when we stand, we let our bodies announce to the world that we are redeemed. We did not redeem ourselves, and that's why our eyes are fixed ahead to the source of our hope—the voice of Christ who speaks in the Gospels and the presence of Christ in the Host that we are to receive upon our lips. And when we leave the church building, we must let this be our attitude toward all existence—remembering our dignity as a redeemed and beloved sons and daughters of the Father.

Sitting is the posture during the Mass that we may be almost too familiar with. When we sit on our couch, we tend to adopt a relaxed and fundamentally passive posture. We sit when we watch a movie, a play, or a football game. We are spectators in such sitting rather than active participants. When we sit at Mass, therefore, we may be tempted to think to ourselves, "Okay, my part is done. Now it's time to relax a bit and let other people do their thing."

But that's not an active approach to sitting. Think about how a bride or a groom sits in a chair in the moments before exchanging vows. Their posture tends not to be passive but expectant. Their feet are on the floor. They may be sitting on the edge of their seat, awaiting the moment in which they pledge their life to their future spouse. Every word that is uttered on this day, the bride and groom are attentive to.

This is the kind of sitting that the liturgy should inspire in us. Reverent sitting should, like standing, be expectant. We sit to listen to the divine Word in sacred scripture. We sit as the gifts are brought toward the altar. The more relaxed posture of sitting demands from us attention to what is unfolding before us so that we may contemplate it. The spoken word. This procession of gifts. A moment of silence before the concluding prayer at Mass. Expectant sitting involves having two feet on the ground. Our eyes may be closed as we listen to scripture to better savor what is proclaimed. But such sitting is a posture of active receptivity, better to receive and delight in the word that is received.

The movement between these postures, something experienced week in and week out at the Sunday liturgy, slowly disposes us to enter into prayer, not despite, but through what we do with our bodies. When we pray at home, we may find ourselves kneeling first because that act of kneeling is itself already a prayer, an occasion of adoration. We sit with eyes closed after we meditate upon a psalm because that very gesture is already an occasion of meditation upon the Lord's word to us. We stand up while praying the Our Father as a family, expressing the dignity proper to the sons and daughters of God.

In all of this, we are practicing something fundamental to our hope. For we Christians dare to proclaim each week the resurrection of the body. When our bodies are raised from the dead, we will no longer experience the kind of limitations that we endure as mortal creatures. Instead, every dimension of our beings will be ordered toward worship. In heaven, praise will no longer be work, a matter of attuning ourselves to God. Worship will be second nature to us. Our whole selves will worship God as easily as we raise a pinky finger or blink our eyes. We will become an act of praise. Birds sing. Bears catch salmon. Human beings adore the living God. It is what we are made for.

So, even now, as we pray at Mass, we are practicing who we will be when we see God face-to-face in the beatific vision, in the resurrection of the dead. We are creatures made entirely for praise—right now, in anticipation; then, in reality.

For now, kneel in humble wonder. Stand with confident hope. Sit in expectant desire for union with God. Practice the gestures of the citizens of heaven.

Behold, Believe, Become

1. Kneeling, standing, and sitting are postures by which we take up a prayerful disposition at Mass. Think about how you take up these postures during the Eucharistic liturgy. Do you do so reverently? With the kind of awareness described in this meditation? If so, how? If not, what would you need to change?

2. What we do with our bodies is linked to the quality of our prayer at Mass, while also preparing us to stand before Christ in our resurrected bodies. How does this insight change the way that you think about prayer?

3. In the context of prayer (whether you're praying the scriptures, the Rosary, or celebrating the Liturgy of the Hours), be more intentional with your bodily postures. Take time to kneel, stand, or sit attentively during your times of prayer this week. Pay attention to how adopting such postures changes the way that you participate at Mass.

Scan this code or visit **http://www.avemariapress.com/behold-believe-become-videos** to watch a video from Tim O'Malley and the Bulman family on meeting Christ in our kneeling, standing, and sitting.

11.

CANDLELIGHT AND INCENSE

There's a special comfort in sitting around a campfire. Even on the hottest of summer days, as the sun descends, the campfire functions like a magnet, drawing people to pause for a moment near its light. We gather around the fire to tell stories, to poke at the fire with a stick, or simply to savor the warmth. The flames leap. The wood crackles. We add new fuel to the fire, until the last log burns, and it's time to settle into our tents—all as the smell of smoke wafting in the air acts as a sensory remembering of what has unfolded that evening at the hearth.

In radical contrast to such cozy warmth, we forget at our own peril how quickly the delight of a campfire can become an agent of ferocious destruction. A single spark, left untended, can enfold dry trees in fiery flames. Houses can disappear into a furnace of devastation. In war, fire is both a comfort for soldiers and a weapon to yield against one's enemies.

It's strange that we let this uncontrollable element into our churches, employing it for the act of divine worship.

Yes, fire can burn down a church. But it can light a candle representing the hidden prayers of an unknown soul. Fire can kill. But it can also be used in the peaceful Eucharistic sacrifice, a lit coal converting incense into a sacramental sign of the fragrant supplications of Christ's people.

Maybe there's something about the uncontrollability of fire that is quite appropriate for Christian worship. For is it not true that we, too, are creatures who can provide warmth and also burn? Who can create a home for the stranger in need but who can also ignore such needs, going on our merry way without the slightest concern for our brother or sister's suffering? Who can adore the living God, but who can also turn toward the worship of power, prestige, fame, and fortune? We love, and we hate. Left to our devices, we can do good beyond belief. We can also enact astonishing harm.

To burn right, we human beings need to let our flames be directed toward the proper object. Thousands of burning candles manifest the power of fire to let Christ's light shine into the darkest of places. One single fiery coal applied to incense creates an aromatic icon of the Church's prayers ascending into the heavens. One human being, consecrated to Christ through Baptism, can become a fiery light of hope for the world.

If our fiery selves are to be a source of light and heat for the world, then we must let our existence be dedicated to the act of worship. Look closely at the flame of a candle. Its sole purpose is to burn and therefore create light for all to behold. The lit coal burns the incense through and through, holding nothing back. We mere mortals must do the same. In the Church's Eucharistic sacrifice, God is asking for our total selves to be dedicated to this act of divine worship, with nothing held back.

If you have a grudge against your neighbor, let that be purified through the fire of divine love. If you are anxious about your future, bring such fretting to the Supper of the Lamb. If your charity has grown cold, your desire for God lacking, let your heart be ignited anew by the words of our Eucharistic Lord: *This is my body, given for you. This is my blood, poured out for you.* For *you.*

Fortunately, you don't have to do this all by yourself. You are part of a cloud of smoky witnesses who have surrendered their whole selves to worship Christ. Go into an old church and smell the centuries of incense that seem to have become part of the very walls. Look at the wax that has overcome the candelabra, notice the smoke stains upon the statue of Our Lady, and see the prayers of generations who have come before you. You are not alone, but one single flame burning in harmonious concert with all those blistering saints (and not a few lukewarm sinners) who have tried to hand everything over to the Lord.

The task of the Christian in worship, therefore, is to become like the inflamed candle or the smoky incense. Yet unlike either the candle or the incense, the fire of charity in the saint burns unceasingly. It is never exhausted but grows brighter and higher and all the more luminous through the gifts of the Spirit. This is why we pray at each Pentecost for the Holy Spirit, the fiery love of God, to descend and warm these frozen hearts of ours. Even if we are inflamed with divine love, regular churchgoers in love with the Eucharistic Lord, our hearts must still seem so cold compared to the burning charity of the triune God, devoid of that smoky fragrance of aromatic incense.

The next time you're at Mass and see that candle or perceive the scent of that incense, pay a bit more attention. Our Lord is inviting you to become fierier, more luminous, a light to the nations, and a superbly fragrant offering of divine love. Hold nothing back; let the Spirit descend and set you on fire.

After all, fire is uncontrollable. And so are all the saints who have left their smoky marks on history—bringing into the world freedom, liberation, and communion made possible through Christ. For it was in Jesus Christ that the flame of his divine essence purified our frigid flesh. And we mortals, sealed with the anointing of the Spirit, now have been immersed in the divine fire of Christ. All Christians who let their hearts be renewed through this worship (offering themselves as sons and daughters back to the Father of all light) may become furnaces of divine warmth wherever they go.

We may just set the world on fire. How marvelously uncontrollable this could be!

Behold, Believe, Become

1. Look very closely the next time you're at Mass at a burning candle or at the incense that rises up into the heavens. What do you notice? What do you think the candle shows you about your own proper way of relating to God?

2. We human beings can become agents of God's fiery warmth if we give our full selves over to the Eucharistic Lord. What are you holding back right now that keeps you from this total gift of self? Where do you need to burn more fragrantly with the power of God's own charity?

3. In the evenings in your home, as you pray before bed, light a candle. Sit in silence before this candle for five minutes, taking in its warmth and light. Only then begin to offer your prayers. Notice how this act of beholding changes the quality of your prayer.

Scan this code or visit **http://www.avemariapress.com/behold-believe-become-videos** to watch a video from Tim O'Malley and the Bulman family on meeting Christ in fire and smoke.

12.

HANDS

We describe eyes as the windows to the soul, those bodily members that give us access to the interior life of another person. Surely, this is true, as any lover knows. We remember the first time we looked into the eyes of our beloved and recognized in this crossing of the gazes, not an object, but a person calling us out of ourselves toward the beloved-to-be. *I love you with all my being.*

In all of this praise of the eye, though, let's not forget the mediating role of the hands. You've surely met people who talk with their hands, whose every word is anticipated by some gesture they make. If someone holds up both hands to you, while walking backward, it should be clear that they want nothing to do with you. When a young child grabs your hand while walking across a street, he isn't just listening to his parents (who told him to do just that). He's saying, "I trust you. I'm handing my safety over to you."

If eyes are the windows to the soul, then hands are the very soul of the person reaching out to make physical contact with the world. Isn't that really the marvelous dimension of the sense of touch? Yes, we can smell something, but that act of sniffing leads to no deeper intimacy with the object (and if it smells bad, it might lead us to run away, rather than come closer). Sight, while often leading us to take some object or person into our mind, still has a certain distance. We see something, but we might be rather far away from it. The same with hearing: just because we hear the footsteps of some hidden creature in the woods doesn't mean we have encountered that creature. Taste consists of a momentary intimacy with food, but our saliva eventually dissolves whatever edible object we were enjoying. But touch is different. It is flesh touching flesh—some world out there entering into our own world.

You can receive this world, though, or you can reject it. Someone extends her hand to you in an act of friendship. You could receive this gesture, or you can coolly give a head nod, denoting your lack of interest in such intimacy. A fork in the right hand may be an invitation to dine with you, but it could also be used to stab someone. The former says, "Welcome"; the latter says, "Back off."

All of this makes our hands rather essential to our worship of God. Sacramental worship throughout Christian history has involved the use of hands. The Spirit is called upon not through mere word but through the laying on of hands. Parents trace the Sign of the Cross upon the foreheads of their children. Oil is applied to those very same foreheads through the hands of the minister. The priest lifts up with his hands the Eucharistic presence of our Lord to behold.

Even for us laypeople, what we do with our hands at Mass matters. If we clasp our hands together in a gesture of prayer, thumbs crossed over each other, we assume a posture toward God of fidelity. If we open our hands up while praying, perhaps even lifting them up to God, we are making ourselves available to the work of the Spirit. If our hands are united almost in a fist, our fingers pressed upon our knuckles, we reveal the fervency of our desire for God's graceful intercession in our lives.

At the same time, if we pay no attention to our hands, if we assume no posture of prayer with these appendages, we are closing ourselves off from God. Yes, we do want a bit of God in our lives, but just enough that we can keep control. We don't want to be viewed as some sort of fervent loon, too serious about religious activity. That's why we cross our arms at Mass instead of assuming the childish posture of the praying hands. *Let's get on with this frivolous business of worship, so we can return to the serious business of living.*

Likely few people think about these things as they thoughtlessly use their hands in worship. But matter matters and, therefore, what we do with our bodies is just as much a part of our worship of God as what we think about or say. If we want to take the Mass more seriously, if we want to learn to pray, we might start with the hands.

What a story, after all, the hands tell. Look down sometime at your hands (especially those of us who have aged a bit), and take notice of what you see. Likely, you see small scars from wounds that have taken place throughout your life. As you get older, you notice the way that your hands—one of the few appendages of your body directly always available to your sight without the use of a mirror—have become more wrinkled. If you touch your left hand to your right, you notice the softness that once characterized your hands as a child is no longer there. Too many dishes done. Too many rough days working in the yard.

When we go to Mass and offer our hands to God in prayer, we are handing over that whole life story to the Father through the Son in the unity of the Holy Spirit. There's a famous prayer of St. Ignatius of Loyola, one that says the following:

> Take, Lord, and receive all my liberty, my memory, my understanding,
> and my entire will, all I have and call my own.
>   You have given all to me.
> To you, Lord, I return it.

Yes, our whole life story (even the difficult moments) is part of God's primordial gift to us. Everything we possess has come from God, who is the source of all we have received. Our freedom. Our story. Our thoughts. Our ability to desire. All have come from God. So, what do we need to do? Give it all back. *My freedom, my story, my thoughts, and my desire—I give them to you, God.*

In fact, this is the very posture that we should assume if we are to receive the Eucharistic presence of our Lord in our hands. Before the Second Vatican Council, people did not receive the Eucharist in this manner but only on the tongue. They knelt and received at a Communion rail that separated the sanctuary from the nave.

But the reformed rites allow for Communion in the hand if the bishops give permission. In the United States, they have. We should, though, be very attentive at how we receive the Eucharistic Lord in these hands. We should not grasp for the Eucharist, taking it with one hand. We should not thoughtlessly plop our hands out as if we're being given some token or trinket. It is the Lord of heaven and earth who comes to dwell among us, who gives himself to us.

So, place one hand underneath the other, slightly curving the hand that is on top. Gently receive the Eucharistic Lord as if your hands are a throne. Now tenderly move the hand on bottom to take the Body of Christ in the fingers of the hand that was on the bottom. Don't do this quickly. Be intentional. Then place the Body of Christ in your mouth. Don't walk back to your pew as if you just got in a line to receive a ticket to some concert. As you walk back, let your hands assume a prayerful posture, folded and fervent. As you sit down in the pew, open your hands up and look at the palms of these appendages. Remember with wonder that the Lord came close to you, to dwell with you under the sign of bread in these very hands. Prayerfully ask God to accept the only offering you can make in return—your whole self.

As Mass ends, there will be other things to do with these hands. Hungry mouths to feed, food to pick, clothes to clean, and the sick to care for. There are neighbors to meet, and folks from the parish with whom we can cooperate hand in hand for the sake of Christ's kingdom on earth. Having received the Eucharistic Lord, these hands must now operate according to the gift they have received, open and graciously receiving all that comes their way. And in that receiving, there will be more and more to give.

It's like hands catching water that descends from a waterfall—hands filled to the brim with divine grace. But you can't hold tightly onto water—or divine grace, for that matter. It will spill right out. Instead, only by assuming and keeping a posture of openness, of gift, can you continue to receive what is given. And in turn, offer what you have received back to God as a gift—the gift of yourself back to God. *To you, Lord, I return it.*

Behold, Believe, Become

1. Whatever time of day you pray best, sit down and be silent for several moments. Then, before saying anything, put your hands into the prayer posture, fingers erect and against one another, thumbs crossed. Close your eyes.

What do you notice about your relationship with God through this posture? Now do the same, except with open hands extended and lifted up to God. What do you notice here?

2. What do you think about the idea that the hands are the soul reaching out to contact the world? What would this mean for how you pray using your hands at Mass?

3. We encountered a prayer from St. Ignatius of Loyola related to surrendering all things to God. Think for a moment of all the gifts that you have received from God, even emerging out of difficult things that have happened to you. Now lift your hands up to God and give thanks for all that you have received, pledging to do nothing more than give yourself in return. Keep doing this for a week, and notice how your way of relating to the world has changed.

Scan this code or visit **http://www.avemariapress.com/behold-believe-become-videos** to watch a video from Tim O'Malley and the Bulman family on meeting Christ with our hands.

13.

EATING AND DRINKING

There are different types of eating and drinking, at least, qualitatively. If you are rushing from one meeting to another, you might stuff a sandwich in your mouth along the way. Eating and drinking becomes a way to refuel, to gain the energy necessary to keep on keeping on. It is the kind of refreshment done by animals and human beings alike who need to slake their hunger and thirst. Eating and drinking are nutrition.

There is the mindless eating that might unfold while anxiously awaiting friends to show up at a party. You're not really hungry. But you feel awkward. So, you go over to a table filled with food and consume tortilla chips and guacamole. If your food was ripped from your hands at this moment, you wouldn't be angry about the loss of food. You wouldn't be famished or dry-throated from thirst. You would simply be annoyed that now the only thing left to do was to chit-chat with strangers. Eating and drinking are comforts.

There is the eating of the gourmand for whom every bite should be savored. Yes, you might be dining with guests, but that's not the reason you waited nine months to go to this restaurant. You're here to enjoy every last bite and sip of food and drink that you can. All along, the gourmand is measuring the quality of the food. Is this wine as good as the 2015 from Bordeaux? Does this steak rise to the level of a Michelin star, or is it more akin to what you can find at your all-you-can-eat buffet? Eating and drinking are savoring.

There is also the eating and drinking that leisurely unfolds in the context of banquets. The food doesn't need to be fancy. But it does need to take time. What's the rush? *Here, guests, consume this course first. Now, have a bit of this wine. Wait, there's another course and more wine!* At a banquet or feast, the conversation and conviviality are as much a part of the meal as the act of eating. Eating and drinking are festive.

Undoubtedly, you the reader might be able to think of other ways of eating. But what has been set forth is enough to consider something essential to our embodied participation in the Eucharist. The Mass leads us to an act of eating and drinking; and yet, it is an act of eating and drinking very different from any other kind we do—for we eat and therefore enter into union with God as we receive the Body and Blood of Christ. Yet how might these various types of eating also be fulfilled in our reception of Holy Communion?

Before continuing, though, a common and particularly thorny objection must be treated. Namely, the focus on the Mass as a meal or banquet has distracted from the reverence that should be our fundamental disposition in the sacrifice of the Mass. When we direct our attention to the meal, the human community instead of God becomes the focal point. We gather around the table of the Lord to eat and drink. The community receives nourishment. But the vertical aspect of communion with God is not attended to. All that is left is the community.

Certainly, such impoverished accounts of the Eucharist as meal have been taken up over the last fifty years since the Second Vatican Council. We hear it in hymns. We encounter it in preaching. We see it in the presiding style of some priests, who act more like a host at a tawdry banquet than as a presider over sacred rites.

But it can go wrong the other way too. It did and has! Before the twentieth century, the faithful were hesitant to partake of the sacred Eucharistic meal. Generations of popes, bishops, and theologians tried to convince people to receive the Eucharistic elements, to eat and drink. St. Albert the Great wrote a whole treatise on the theological meaning of eating and drinking (and digestion) around the Eucharist. One of St. Thomas Aquinas's most famous antiphons is *O sacrum convivium*—O sacred banquet.

The division between meal and sacrifice in relation to the Mass is one of those infamous either/ors, rather than the Catholic both/ands. Throughout the Bible, sacred meals are sacrifices. And sacrifices are related to the act of eating and drinking. There's a reason that Jesus Christ institutes the Eucharist in the context of the Passover meal, a meal inexplicably linked to sacrifice. The sacrifice of the lamb, whose blood was put on the doorposts, led to the liberation of Israel from the powers and principalities of the Egyptians. Similarly the sacrifice of the Lamb of God once slain is understood as the new Passover. And on the night before he died, Christ told us to do this sacrificial meal in his memory.

So, the Mass is a meal. It is a weird one, of course. The food isn't plentiful. We Catholics profess that the signs of bread and wine remain (and, therefore, they taste and act like those elements), but they are now the personal presence of Jesus Christ. They are our Lord, given to us under these signs in a way that we can receive him. No other meal offers this.

But because it is a meal, the materiality of eating and drinking remains a way of contemplating the mystery. To do so isn't to say, "Hey, Jesus isn't really present in the Eucharist." It isn't to say, "Hey, do whatever you want. The Church is basically just running a really terrible bakery." But rather, contemplating the materiality of bread and wine tells us that the Lord wants to intimately unite himself to us through the act of eating and drinking. This really matters.

So, the Eucharist is a moment of nutrition. Rather than lead to a sufficient intake of calories, vitamins, or minerals, the Eucharist gives grace. Grace means gift—in Latin, *gratia*. What is the gift? It is God himself, who comes to feed us. There are all sorts of things that we can hunger and thirst for. Food. Booze. Sex. Fortune. Self-importance. If you want to add more, just read the news. But the only thing that can slake our hunger is the gift of God himself, who comes to us. The Eucharist, as has already been noted, is the weirdest food and drink. We're eating God (under the signs of bread and wine). But how can we eat God? We can't. God is God, and you don't eat God. Rather, as St. Augustine notes, it is God who eats us. We enter into God's life. So, the nutrition that is given as we eat and drink the Body and Blood of Christ is the grace of divine life. The gift of divine life. The gift of God. What else could feed us?

The Eucharist is a moment of comfort. The awkwardness you feel at a party is normal. You don't feel at home. So, while you're waiting, you eat and drink. Guess what? None of us are at home. We are all that awkward person at a party. For we are made for something more, for a union with God that transcends anything we can construct on our own. That's why we so often feel at dis-ease in this world. You get the job of your dreams, and you don't feel totally happy. You buy the house you always wanted, but it doesn't complete you. You meet your life's companion, and you still think to yourself, *Is this enough?* The answer is no, it's not. You are made for union with God. All happiness here in this world, therefore, is but a foretaste of happiness to come. The Eucharist is a foretaste of eternal life, a hint of the heaven to come. But in that sense, in eating and drinking the Body and Blood of Christ, we are receiving comfort. *One day, this will be your whole life. You will feast on God's presence. But for now, take this little morsel.* That is why there isn't too much given in the Eucharist. Just a bit of what looks like bread. A sip of what was once wine. That's all. If you want more after the Eucharist, good. Long for union with God.

The Eucharist is a gourmand's dream. Not because the signs of bread and wine are all that splendid. They're actually rather austere. Typically, the worst of unleavened bread is used. The Communion wine used at Mass: you're probably not going to find it in *Wine Spectator*'s Best of the Year. It's all so ordinary. But that belies the really extraordinary thing we are invited to savor. Here comes the Lord, giving himself to us. You don't see it or taste it. But it is the God-man, his divine life, that comes to dwell in your heart. The only access you have to this mystery is faith. Contemplate in faith what you are eating and drinking. Medieval theology often spoke of the act of meditation as chewing. You have to let the flavors of the mystery really seep into your bones, slowly, likely throughout your life. As you eat and drink the Body and Blood of Christ under the signs of bread and wine, you must savor that mystery. Here, our Lord gives himself to you. You, suffering from cancer. You, abused by a priest of the Church. You, someone dealing with a dead-end job. The mystery you can, should, might savor is the gift of love given in the Eucharist. God wants to be close to you in the Eucharist, no matter how joyful your joys are or how sorrowful your sorrows are. When you receive the Eucharist, consume the Host slowly. Not because eating the Eucharist will crush our Lord! That's not what the Church teaches. But because you're invited to savor the sweetness of our Lord, who wants to be with you.

A side note: maybe you're in a diocese that has not restored the chalice since the pandemic (and if you're reading this in 2122, who knows what pandemic we're talking about?). I know this is a further point of contention in the Church. Should the lay faithful receive the chalice? Was that a good addition after the Second Vatican Council? The US bishops officially teach, yes, it is worth it. We have a special instruction on reception under both species. The chalice is part of savoring the mystery. St. Thomas Aquinas once said it is fitting that wine be used in the Eucharist, because wine is intended to gladden the hearts of men and women. Wine is sweet. Wine delights. It gladdens our hearts. So, our Lord gives himself to us under the signs of that gift. You don't have to receive the chalice, but the delight of drinking such sweetness leads us to understand the Eucharist anew.

The Eucharist is a feast. After all, we're not eating and drinking by ourselves. There is a temptation in Eucharistic piety to forget this fact. *It's my individual Communion, and to hell (literally) with the rest of you.* The Eucharistic feast, though, is intended to bring about conviviality. Not just with those gathered in the parish that day. That's the kind of bad, horizontal communion we addressed above. No, the communion is with the living and the dead. The rich and the poor. The saints and the sinners. We are invited to the greatest of all banquets, one that anticipates heaven itself—where all sinners will be purified to become saints, and all saints will be all the more holy. I eat next to you, with you. My reception of Communion and your reception and all those receptions are linked to one another.

And the thing is, there's room at this banquet. Look at your parish; you haven't invited everyone yet. You know those who feel they don't belong because they are suffering from mental illness. There's room at the feast. You know those who have an intellectual disability, who are regularly excluded by the wider social body. There's room. Men and women of every color. Men and women of every socioeconomic level. There's room.

And there's room not because we have constructed some utopian social body. We are bad at such things. Our utopian social orders tend to exclude those who are not part of the mainstream. *All are welcome, except the libs. Except the conservatives. Except the Trump supporters or the Biden apologists. Get out.*

No! The banquet is at hand. And the host is also the meal. It is the God-man, Jesus Christ, who came to invite all men and women to the banquet. Yes, those invited have to change their lives. Who doesn't? The feast that we're celebrating is that God is love, love unto the end. A love that requires us to forgive the one who has offended, to cease being hypocrites, to give our cheek to the enemy, and to commit ourselves to friendship with the poor. Utopian societies would fail at that (and they will keep failing at that, because they build their societies not out of divine grace but out of bureaucracy and statecraft). But if the Lord gathers us, invites us to this banquet, feeds us with his very self, there's some hope.

So, come to the sacrificial banquet. The victim and the host are the same. It is the Lamb once slain, who unites us with his beating heart of love. Receive your nutrition. Delight in the comfort. Savor the mystery. Anticipate the banquet. And come back next week. But invite a new guest. Our host and victim is partial to that.

Behold, Believe, Become

1. The Eucharist is the Body and Blood, soul and divinity of Christ. But our Lord gives himself to us under the signs of bread and wine for eating and drinking. Pay attention to how you think about eating and drinking. What do you think you might learn about the Eucharist from your natural attitudes toward food and drink?

2. Although the Eucharist is the strangest of foods, our Lord feeds us, providing nutrition, comfort, delight, and a convivial banquet. Which one of these ways of eating are you most attracted to? Which do you struggle with?

3. St. Thomas Aquinas has a beautiful antiphon, called the *O sacrum convivium*, which translated is "O sacred banquet / in which Christ is received / the memory of his

passion is recalled / the mind is filled with grace / and a pledge of future glory is given. / Alleluia." Memorize this antiphon. Say it to yourself each time you come to receive our Lord in the Eucharist. Pay attention to how your attitude of receiving Christ under the signs of bread and wine changes as you "chew" upon this antiphon.

Scan this code or visit **http://www.avemariapress.com/behold-believe-become-videos** to watch a video from Tim O'Malley and the Bulman family on meeting Christ in eating and drinking.

14.

SILENCE

As with eating and drinking, there are different types of silence. The silence of a grudge against a friend where speechlessness is the chasm that separates the two parties from each other. The silence of an early relationship where the couple is just getting used to being in each other's presence without a cascade of words. The dreadful silence that fills the examination room between the doctor's "I have bad news" and "It's cancer." The predawn silence in a mountain cabin as the sun begins to illuminate the foothills on a summer morning.

What's interesting about our age is that we are not all that good at most types of silence. We schlep around digital devices that make sounds, entertaining and distracting us from all occasions of noiseless boredom. We are a society that eschews both visual and auditory silence. Get on a plane sometime and look at your fellow passengers. If they are traveling alone, they'll be watching videos. Surfing the web. Texting with friends. They likely won't be sitting in silence, looking out the window, wondering at the world around them.

And yet such silence is essential to human happiness. To really understand the necessity of silence, you have to think about musical notation. Even in the most fulsome symphonic setting, there are places in the music where there are rests. The composer is telling the musician not to play here, because that moment of rest is a buildup to what follows. It is part of the dance of it all, from silence to music and back again.

Our discomfort with silence is, I fear, an uneasiness with solitude. We don't want silence, because we don't want to be alone. We don't want to enter that interior space of our souls where there is nothing except the self. Asking questions. Coming to insights. Dreaming and pondering a future.

Our unease with the silence of solitude carries over into the Mass. A typical parish Eucharistic liturgy is full of unnecessary noise. I'm not talking about the noise of babbling children (may that joyful sound increase all the more). Rather, I mean the noise of words that do not need to be said. The noise of an efficiency that cannot pause for a moment, giving the assembly an occasion to enter into solitude. The cantor has an announcement that doesn't need to be made. The priest inserts additional words that do not need to be said. The choir makes more music than is necessary, giving no one a chance to be alone with the Beloved.

The shame of it all is that the assembly doesn't get to experience one of the most remarkable silences in the human condition—the silence of a gathered crowd. On September 11, 2001, I was a student at the University of Notre Dame when we heard about the collapse of the Twin Towers, the plane crash in Pennsylvania, and the attack on the Pentagon.

School was canceled. More than eleven thousand people gathered that very afternoon on South Quad for Mass. That ninety-minute Mass was marked by silence. Saying too much didn't seem right, didn't fit the situation. We had nowhere to be, nothing to do, except to sit there in the grass and pray for those who died. Eleven thousand people gathered, not to make noise, but to be silent with one another—to be silent before God.

And yes, liturgical silence is ultimately ordered toward letting God speak, giving God space to act. It is the expectant silence of Holy Saturday when the Church waits for the Resurrection of the Lord. It is the pregnant silence of Pentecost Sunday when the disciples gather in the upper room, longing for the descent of the Spirit. Silence is giving God the space to be God.

After receiving our Lord in the Eucharist, this is the kind of silence that is appropriate. God has come to dwell among us. We are united with Christ, nourished by his Eucharistic presence. After all the words that we have said in the Eucharistic liturgy, all the speech we have listened to, each of us is alone, together with the Beloved. We wait for him to speak, giving him the space to act in our life.

You can see how discomfort with silence at Mass is really fear of being alone with God. That's bad news. If you're a parent, you surely have had the terrifying experience of being alone with a toddler who wants nothing more than to be with you. That's the only thing that the toddler wants. The toddler doesn't particularly care about your ability to answer emails or multitask. She just wants you to be there as she builds, knocks down, and rebuilds a tower out of wooden blocks. Hours could pass doing this, hours spent in silence.

God is like the toddler in our lives who wants nothing more than our presence. God is not looking for our resumes, for us to create some fancy speech that proves our religious commitment. God wants us, and in that intimate encounter following the reception of his Body and Blood, we are called to be silent before the One who desires us.

If we're going to learn to be comfortable with silence at Mass, we will need to practice being alone. We need to practice not looking at our phones, being distracted by the visual and sonic alike. Most of all, we need to work on our desires. Do we desire nothing more than being alone before God, remaining close to our beloved Lord?

Our discomfort with this kind of solitude is an invitation toward a deeper religious conversion. Yes, our prayer must involve words. Prayer and ritual action go together too. But if that's all we do, if that's our sole focus, it may be because we are afraid of letting God into our lives. The words and the ritual acts and announcements at the end of Mass are then talismans warding off an encounter with an awesome God who wants to spend time with us, to waste away eternity with us.

True silence is inefficient. It's not going to get anything done. But it is the kind of silence that feeds the soul, leading us to a foretaste of heavenly bliss. We must learn at Mass to be more comfortable with the saving gravity of such silence before the mystery of the living God.

Behold, Believe, Become

1. Pay attention to the moments over the course of a day in which you experience total silence. How many are there? How many times over the course of the day did you choose distraction over silence (for example, looking at your phone in line at the grocery store rather than just standing there)? Why did you choose distraction over silence and wondering?

2. Our reluctance to experience common silence at Mass is linked to our fear of solitude before God. Are you afraid of this solitude? If so, why? If not, why not?

3. Make a commitment over the course of a month to spend fifteen minutes in totally silent prayer each day. Don't use a book. Don't pray the Rosary. You can use a holy image to focus your attention. But that's it. After a month of doing this, assess how comfortable you are with silent prayer. How has this type of prayer changed the way that you participate in the Mass?

Scan this code or visit **http://www.avemariapress.com/behold-believe-become-videos** to watch a video from Tim O'Malley and the Bulman family on meeting Christ in silent stillness.

15.

RECESSION

Taking leave is fundamental to the human condition. We go to school, then we graduate, leaving that educational institution and the people behind. We visit with a friend, experiencing the delight of communion, and then it's time to go home. We enter into this world as a little creature, fresh from our mother's womb, and yet we are moving (whether we want to or not) toward leaving it all behind at the moment of our death.

At the end of Mass, we also leave. Yes, there is a procession out of the building featuring candles and a crucifix. Likely, there is some sort of closing song. There may even be that post-Eucharistic bread for the journey most important to the child: donuts. But after all that has happened, after the august words are spoken and prayed, we leave. Mass has ended. Go in peace.

Now, we probably don't want to think about it, but it may be beneficial to recognize upon our leaving the church building that this could be our *last* Mass. It could be the final time we celebrate the Eucharist. Before we come back next Sunday, we may embark upon our final leave. We may be dead.

In the ancient world, this practice of thinking about one's death was known as *memento mori*, remembering death. It was a philosophical practice intended to help you reorder your desires. If today is your last day on earth, suddenly the fight you had with your neighbor this morning or the ten emails that you needed to send before leaving work may not seem all that important. If death is at hand, how would you live differently now?

So, as you're leaving the Mass, the task at hand is to wonder how you're going to live differently, as if this were the final time you would receive the Body and Blood of Christ. The last time you would pray the Eucharistic Prayer as a member of the living. How are you going to change from this encounter *now*, recognizing that all of us are contingent creatures whose time on earth is shorter than we might want?

If you start thinking this way when you leave Mass, you will probably come to a deeper awareness of the really serious task that we Christians undertake in this world. Did you feed the hungry and give drink to the thirsty? Did you pardon (or ask for pardon from) your neighbor? Have you taught and proclaimed the Gospel in difficult situations? Have you shared all things in common, embracing voluntary poverty?

These are the questions that must haunt the one leaving the church building on a Sunday morning. For this Mass was not just a bit of peace and quiet intended to serve as a momentary interlude to the workaday world. Rather, it was a bodily enactment of the sacramental vocation to sanctify the cosmos. Everything can be consecrated back to the Father; therefore, while the Mass ends, the Eucharistic vocation of the Christian continues.

The awareness of this vocation, though, necessitates the very kind of "seeing" that we learned to practice at Mass. We're often too busy or distracted to notice those areas where we are called to live as one transformed by the Eucharistic mystery. We create a partition between our Eucharistic self and the rest of our life. Mass is one thing; work and family are different. Yes, we could feed or recognize that hungry man who stands on our street corner. But there's so much to do, so little time.

A foolish decision, for alas, we only have this body. We only have this life. And that's the life that we are called to offer as a living sacrifice back to the Father. A personal sacrifice of our entire self.

What modern religiosity has taught us is to separate the act of worship from everything else. Worship is private. Politics is public. Adoration is private. Economics is public. Do whatever you want in the private sphere, but don't bring it to the public one. Worship the Eucharistic Lord, but don't you dare let it affect how you think about politics, economics, education, or anything else.

We can't think like this. It's not an option for those of us consecrated to Jesus Christ through our Baptism, confirmed in the Spirit, and fed by the hand of the Lord. Our washing of dishes, our feeding of our kids, our counseling of the doubtful, the way that we treat our coworkers, our care for the unborn child and his mother, our visiting of the prisoner—these are all embodied acts of worship that depend upon our leave-taking at the end of Mass. And we only have a bit of time to do this kind of worship.

So, as you leave Mass, remember that you won't be alive forever. You are moving toward your final recession not from Mass but from this world. You are dying. And with this fact in mind, reorder your priorities. The change starts with yourself, with a serious examination of your own Eucharistic negligence.

Imagine that you are a busy person, the kind who has so much to do that you barely have time to think. You like to squeeze every drop of productivity out of a day. And you do! But you begin to notice that this is having a deleterious effect on your relationships. You don't really pay attention to your kids, because you're thinking about work. You have stopped admiring your spouse. Your primary attitude toward the world isn't gratitude but anxiety. The time to change is now! Start being grateful. Adopt practices that allow you to spend time with those whom you love. You probably won't regret these decisions, I suspect. No one, on their deathbed, is accompanied by the CEO of their company. It's friends and families, spouses and kids, who are there at the end.

This examination, though, doesn't stop with you. There are wounds in the world that need to be attended to. Many people who belong to our parishes go to bed hungry. Not a few may be suffering from loneliness or depression, perhaps even considering suicide. There are marriages on the rocks often because couples feel as if they have no support. Some of your fellow parishioners are in precarious jobs, afraid that they might lose their only source of income for reasons outside of their control. Kids are suffering from anxiety, from the impossible standards that their elders have set up for them. If you knew this was your last day on earth, if you could reorder how you spent your time, wouldn't you at least try to do something to help these folks?

If you take seriously the limited time you have in this life, your contingency as a creature, then you're going to start getting more out of Mass. You will hunger for the bread from heaven because it nourishes you in the work of social and cultural renewal. You will desire the sacrifice of praise in which you acknowledge your weakness before God and let God's power change you. You will see how the hidden presence of the Beloved in the Eucharistic elements is most fitting, because that's how this hidden God appears in the least of these.

Peter Maurin, who helped found the Catholic Worker, wrote little essays (aptly titled *Easy Essays*). I like to imagine them as thought experiments for those who recognize that they are contingent, dependent, and limited creatures. It's as

if he was thinking for those of us who know we are on the
way to taking our final leave. In one of these thought experiments, Maurin wrote:

> Christianity has not been tried
> because people thought
> it was impractical.
> And men have tried everything
> except Christianity.
> And everything
> that men have tried
> has failed.

If Maurin is right (and I think he is), we have to recognize how impractical Mass and the Eucharist are. They're
impractical because they don't depend on the hard-nosed,
sober logic of the market or the political sphere. The worker
who shows up at the end gets the same amount of money as
someone gainfully employed all day. The kingdom's celeb-
rity is the child, incapable of the kind of duplicity regularly
practiced by those who occupy political office. Fathers extrav-
agantly forgive children who take their inheritance too early,
welcoming them back and throwing a party in their honor.

This is all impractical. It's the impracticality of divine
generosity. And if we want to live out of this sense of gratuity
(and this is what Eucharistic living is really about), we have
to get to dying. Dying to self. Dying from our addiction to
idols. And living for the Lord alone. Everything else has been

tried, hasn't it? Maybe this Eucharistic experiment might, in fact, be crazy enough to work?

It is likely that you have many more Masses before you than the last one you attended. But if you start living as if you didn't, as if this act of leaving the church building were the final time that you would be among the church militant, then ironically your whole life would become a lot like the Mass.

> A sacrifice of praise in which everything is ordered toward Christ.
> A recognition of the presence of the hidden Lord.
> A remembering of the mystery of love in all that you say, think, or do.
> An anticipation of communion with the very charity of God who is in heaven.
> Amen.

Behold, Believe, Become

1. Imagine that you only have six months left to live. How would you start to live differently?

2. The Mass is the privileged way that we Catholics live out our vocation to the Eucharist. But that vocation does not end with the Mass. Where in your life do you need to better integrate your worship of God at Mass with your worship of God in the world? It could be related to

something personal or something more public (for example, how you think about politics, how you spend your money, and so on). What obstacles do you think you might encounter as you move toward this integration?

3. Make a list of the ways that you serve someone in your life on a daily basis. How would you understand this service differently if you saw it as related to your own embodied worship of God at Mass? The next time you're engaged in one of these acts of service, think about it as a moment of worshipping God. Does that change the way that you perform the task?

Scan this code or visit **http://www.avemariapress.com/behold-believe-become-videos** to watch a video from Tim O'Malley and the Bulman family on meeting Christ in leave-taking.

Timothy P. O'Malley is a Catholic theologian, educator, and author at the McGrath Institute for Church Life at the University of Notre Dame. He teaches and researches in the areas of liturgical-sacramental theology, marriage and family, and catechesis. He is especially interested in the question of developing a worshipful wisdom in a culture that has forgotten the art of contemplation, festivity, and communion. He has served in various roles with the USCCB's Eucharistic Revival and the USCCB's Committee on Laity, Marriage, Family Life, and Youth.

O'Malley earned his bachelor's degree in theology and philosophy and his master's degree in theology with a concentration in liturgical studies from the University of Notre Dame. He earned a doctorate in theology and education from Boston College, where he wrote on an Augustinian approach to mystagogy in a secular age.

O'Malley is the author of ten books, including three award-winning books published by Ave Maria Press: *Off the Hook: God, Love, Dating, and Marriage in a Hookup World*; *Real Presence: What Does It Mean and Why Does It Matter?*; and *Becoming Eucharistic People: The Hope and Promise of Parish Life*. He has written for scholarly journals, the McGrath Institute for Church Life's own *Church Life Journal*, and popular magazines throughout the United States.

He lives with his family in the South Bend, Indiana, area.

The McGrath Institute for Church Life was founded as the Center for Pastoral and Social Ministry by the late Notre Dame president Fr. Theodore Hesburgh, CSC, in 1976. The McGrath

Institute partners with Catholic dioceses, parishes, and schools to provide theological education and formation to address pressing pastoral problems. The Institute connects the Catholic intellectual tradition to the pastoral life of the Church in forming faithful Catholic leaders for service to the Church and the world. The McGrath Institute strives to be the preeminent source of creative Catholic content and programming for the new evangelization in the United States.

Watch **FREE** *Behold, Believe, Become* Companion Videos Featuring Deacon Jason and Rachel Bulman

Scan the QR code or visit
avemariapress.com/behold-believe-become-videos.